Children's Book Illustration and Design

Children's Book Illustration and Design

Edited by Julie Cummins

Library of Applied Design

PBC INTERNATIONAL, INC. ✦ NEW YORK

Distributor to the book trade in the United States and Canada:

Rizzoli International Publications Inc.
300 Park Avenue South
New York, NY 10010

Distributor to the art trade in the United States and Canada:

PBC International, Inc.
One School Street
Glen Cove, NY 11542
1-800-527-2826
Fax 516-676-2738

Distributor throughout the rest of the world:

Hearst Books International
1350 Avenue of the Americas
New York, NY 10019

Library of Congress Cataloging-in-Publication Data

Children's book illustration and design / edited by Julie Cummins.
     p.   cm.
    Includes indexes.
    ISBN 0-86636-147-2
    1. Illustrated books, Children's.   2. Illustration of books—20th
century.   3. Illustrators—Biography.   4. Book design.
I. Cummins, Julie.
NC965.C43   1991
741.6'42'09048--dc20   91-31457
                                                                  CIP

CAVEAT—Information in this text is believed accurate, and will pose
no problem for the student or casual reader. However, the author was
often constrained by information contained in signed release forms,
information that could have been in error or not included at all. Any
misinformation (or lack of information) is the result of failure in these
attestations. The author has done whatever is possible to insure
accuracy.

Color separation, printing and binding by
Toppan Printing Co. (H.K.) Ltd. Hong Kong

Typography by
TypeLink, Inc.

Printed in Hong Kong

10 9 8 7 6 5 4 3 2 1

Acknowledgments

One hand does not clap alone. The publication of this book required many hands and I wish to acknowledge the numerous individuals who provided assistance and contributions : publishers, agents, editors, promotion staff, families of illustrators and the illustrators themselves.

There were phone calls, faxes and more phone calls; relatives who searched attics for original art; efforts from foundations and estates to provide materials; hand deliveries of valuable original illustrations; tracking the trail of ownership of rights across the country and the continent. All in all, many hands have helped to shape this book.

Finally, this publication would not have been possible without a cadre of people involved in the children's book world who have a commitment to quality picture books. They recognized the opportunity to share an enthusiasm for spotlighting wonderful and exciting illustrations and illustrators in the world of contemporary children's books which enabled the designing and production of this book. Thanks to each of you and special thanks to Kevin, Susan and Blair.

Contents

Introduction

The phrase "It's all in the way you look at it" is applicable to any art form that employs elements of design. For example, two artists painting the same still life will produce two different pictures and representations. The phrase has particular meaning when applied to the art of children's book illustration where the source for the artwork is the story. Whether it is a folk or fairy tale from centuries past or a contemporary tale created by a writer, the imagery of the illustrator is what brings the story to life and breathes character, mood, and feeling into the book. It is the illustrator's "eye" that produces visual creativity: a child's picture book.

This book is a showcase of outstanding contemporary children's book illustration. Over 80 illustrators are included with illustrations from various books demonstrating an incredible range of styles, techniques and innovation.

The preparation of the book was a multi-step process beginning with the selection of illustrators who were invited to participate. Next came the selection of each individual's books from which illustrations would be replicated. If the artist's work contains more than one medium or style, the choice of books is intended to demonstrate a spectrum. The final decision was made by the individual illustrator who selected the specific illustration to be reproduced from each book. The end result is a combination of selections from the editor's choice and the illustrator's personal judgment, the best of two perspectives.

The illustrators presented are an amalgam of well-known picture book artists and new talent to the field. Many of the artists are award-winning illustrators and represent an international scope. At the time of publication all of the people are actively contributing to children's book publishing with the exceptions of Paul Galdone, Ezra Jack Keats, Arnold Lobel, Martin Provensen, John Steptoe and Margot Zemach. Their work is included because each made significant contributions to the field of contemporary children's books.

The number of children's books that are published annually, approximately 5,000, has increased significantly over the past two decades. New trends bloom and become part of the mainstream or else fade away. The existence of the picture book, defined as a unified blend of pictures and words that together create a whole, has continued to thrive and expand so that it is now an established art form.

The creation of a picture book is the most exciting and challenging area of illustrating children's books. Taking a story that is short in length, conceiving it visually, and applying the aesthetics of line, color and expression is an illustrator's "dream."

The design of a picture book becomes an interplay between the illustrator's interpretation and artistic execution. Composition, color, line, texture and perspective are the design elements the illustrator employs to determine the rhythm, the mood, the flavor, the enactment of what takes place in the book. The illustrator takes the written narrative and translates it into a visual narrative. The achievement of that presentation will utilize the visual effects of balance, variety, emphasis, unity and spatial order—all from the illustrator's explication of the sense of the story. The invisible "inner eye" shapes and molds the story kernel through imagination and creativity into the quintessence of a picture book.

Recognition of children's book illustration is evident in the numerous awards given for the art form. The two most prestigious ones are the Caldecott Award and Greenaway Award. Bestowed annually by the Association for Library Service to Children, a division of the American Library Association, the Caldecott Medal is presented to the artist of the most distinguished American picture book for children. The British counterpart is the Kate Greenaway Medal which is awarded annually by the (British) Library Association to an artist who has produced the most distinguished work in illustration of a children's book. Both medals are named after 19th-century British artists who helped revolutionize children's book illustration: Randolph Caldecott and Kate Greenaway.

Other awards for excellence in illustration include *The New York Times* Best Illustrated Children's Books of the Year, Hans Christian Andersen Awards, International Board on Books for Young People (IBBY) Awards, Biennale of Illustrations Bratislava (BIB), *Boston Globe-Horn Book* Awards and Coretta Scott King Awards.

Many of the illustrators in the showcase are recipients of these awards and their entries cite the honors each has received.

As with all forms of art, appreciation is a matter of personal taste and individual appeal. Child appeal and involvement are significant factors in the designing of picture books. Most of the awards cited above contain child appeal and relationship to child perception in their criteria. There are no hard and fast rules about what constitutes interest by children. Gone are the days when the perception was that everything for young children must be portrayed realistically. As you will see in the following pages, some of the artwork is sophisticated, abstract, or highly stylized. The response from children to these books is enjoyment and fascination with pictures that expand the text and challenge their imagination.

From aardvarks to zebras, from the fantasy of Little Red Riding Hood to the realism of New York City children, the contemporary world of children's book illustration is as exciting and animating as the eye can see or the imagination can soar. Enjoy this panorama of visual narratives. It runs from A to Z, from Allen to Zemach, illustrating the exhilarating, captivating, and creative field of children's book illustration and design.

Julie Cummins

Coordinator, Children's Services
The New York Public Library

Thomas B. Allen

BOOK TITLE
In Coal Country
AUTHOR
Judith Hendershot
ILLUSTRATOR
Thomas B. Allen
PUBLISHER
Alfred A. Knopf
PUBLICATION DATE
1987
ILLUSTRATION MEDIUM
Charcoal and pastel

Thomas B. Allen grew up in Tennessee during the Great Depression. He took his first art course at age nine, attended Vanderbilt University and the School of the Chicago Art Institute where he earned a B.F.A. in painting in 1952. His illustrations have appeared in *Esquire, The New Yorker, Life* and a host of other publications, as well as in numerous distinguished children's books including *In Coal Country* which won both the *Boston Globe-Horn Book* Honor Award and *The New York Times* Best Illustrated Children's Books Award in 1987. Thomas B. Allen is currently the Hallmark Distinguished Professor of Design at the University of Kansas in Lawrence, where he lives with his wife and daughter.

"*A* member of Judith Hendershot's family, after finishing the book, said, 'I feel like I have to wash the coal dust off my hands.'"

"I think that says it all."

BOOK TITLE
On Grandaddy's Farm
AUTHOR
Thomas B. Allen
ILLUSTRATOR
Thomas B. Allen
PUBLISHER
Alfred A. Knopf
PUBLICATION DATE
1989
ILLUSTRATION MEDIUM
Charcoal and pastel

"*The major challenge was writing the story for a picture book with a logical beginning, middle and ending. I wanted to evoke a sense of another time—a simpler time when children had fewer things yet had a lot of fun and did their part, too.*"

Mitsumasa Anno

Mitsumasa Anno grew up in the countryside in a beautiful area of western Japan where he observed nature attentively and learned how to sketch and draw. He also became a first-rate painter. Anno's work reflects the influence of Maurice Escher and incorporates the principles of topology, a branch of mathematics. Many of his books are characterized by a unique intellectual nonsense. Anno's international accolades include the Hans Christian Andersen, Kate Greenaway and *Boston Globe-Horn Book* awards. Domestically, he has received the Minister of Education Award for Encouraging New Talent, the Kodansha Culture Prize for Children's Picture Book Publication, and many other illustrious prizes.

BOOK TITLE
Anno's Medieval World
AUTHOR
Mitsumasa Anno
ILLUSTRATOR
Mitsumasa Anno
PUBLISHER
Philomel Books
PUBLICATION DATE
1980

"*...This book is intended to show that the change from one view of the universe to another was literally an epoch-making change; with it we entered into a new scientific era from an old one which was clouded with superstition....*"

With the plague to fear, and witches, and the devil, the world was a frightening place. But people feared death most of all—for death is stronger than the strongest man.
"We must find the elixir of life," they said, and mixed potions from the bark of trees and from the roots of grass. They looked for it everywhere, in the mountains and beneath the sea, for they hoped, by that means, to conquer death.

BOOK TITLE
Topsy-Turvies
AUTHOR
Mitsumasa Anno
ILLUSTRATOR
Mitsumasa Anno
PUBLISHER
Philomel Books
PUBLICATION DATE
1968

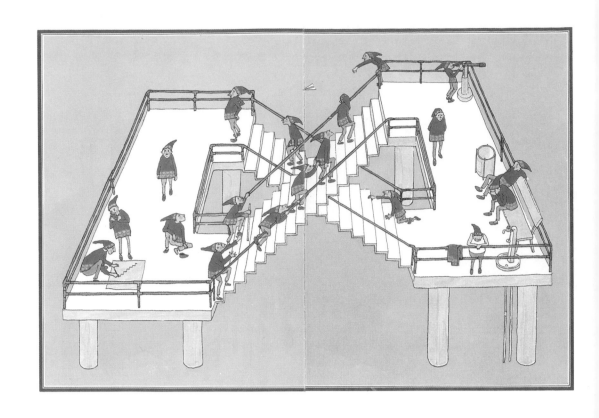

"*I have purposely added no words to these topsy-turvy pictures of mine so you can make them mean whatever you want them to mean.*"

"*Perhaps these pictures of mine will keep all of us young a little longer, will stretch our imaginations enough to help keep us magically human.*"

Jim Arnosky

Artist/naturalist Jim Arnosky began a freelance career in outdoor writing and art at age 24. His work reflects his abiding interest in nature and focuses on the bogs, fields, woods, streams, ponds and hillsides that surround the cities where most people live. Frequently cited for his contributions to children's science literature, Jim Arnosky has garnered awards from the National Science Teachers Association and the New York Academy of Science. In 1991 he received the Eva L. Gordon Award for his body of work contributing to children's science literature, presented by the American Nature Study Society in association with Cornell University. Mr. Arnosky teaches a course on outdoor sketching at Penn State University, where he emphasizes the importance of seeing and understanding over technique, medium or art history. In 1986 he wrote and appeared in the four-part PBS series, "Drawing from Nature," based on his book of the same title.

BOOK TITLE
Freshwater Fish & Fishing
AUTHOR
Jim Arnosky
ILLUSTRATOR
Jim Arnosky
PUBLISHER
Four Winds Press
PUBLICATION DATE
1982
ILLUSTRATION MEDIUM
Gray ink
PHOTOGRAPHER
Bill McConnell

"Fishing is the best activity I can think of to teach ecology and hands-on use of natural resources."

BOOK TITLE
Come Out , Muskrats
AUTHOR
Jim Arnosky
ILLUSTRATOR
Jim Arnosky

PUBLISHER
Lothrop, Lee & Shepard
PUBLICATION DATE
1989
ILLUSTRATION MEDIUM
Watercolor and colored pencil
PHOTOGRAPHER
Bill McConnell

"*My approach to all my pictures is simply to capture a moment in nature in a scene. I like to include motion, and especially environment—such as breezes, sunlight, dust, and water. My books touch on a variety of outdoor subjects, from wildlife to fishing.*"

BOOK TITLE
Deer at the Brook
AUTHOR
Jim Arnosky
ILLUSTRATOR
Jim Arnosky
PUBLISHER
Lothrop, Lee & Shepard
PUBLICATION DATE
1986
ILLUSTRATION MEDIUM
Watercolor and colored pencil
PHOTOGRAPHER
Bill McConnell

"*I must live my work before I write about it. I spend more time outdoors than I do working on the board.*"

Graeme Base

Born in Amersham, England, Graeme Base moved to Melbourne, Australia, in 1966, completed a Diploma of Art in Graphic Design at Swinburne College of Technology in 1978, and briefly pursued a career in advertising. He wrote and illustrated his first picture book, *My Grandma Lived in Gooligulch,* in 1982. Following the publication of *Animalia* in 1986, Mr. Base spent a year traveling throughout the world visiting Thailand, India, Nepal, East Africa, Egypt, Israel, Britain, North America and Japan, during which time he wrote *The Eleventh Hour.* Both *Animalia* and *The Eleventh Hour* won the Young Australian Best Book Award, the Kids Own Australian Literature Award, and both received commendations from the Australian Book Publishers Association.

BOOK TITLE
The Eleventh Hour
AUTHOR
Graeme Base
ILLUSTRATOR
Graeme Base
PUBLISHER
Penguin Books Australia Ltd.
Harry N. Abrams, New York
PUBLICATION DATE
1989
ILLUSTRATION MEDIUM
Inks, gouache and pencil

"I like making pictures that demand close attention so I set out to create a book that would serve as a vehicle for this desire. I decided to make a mystery story in pictures with clues hidden in the illustrations, then spent 1987 traveling, collecting visual ideas. Early on in the year I spent a month in the game parks of Kenya and Tanzania. This is why many of the animals in the book are African. As I traveled I designed the book, influences from India, Egypt and Europe creeping into the pages as I went along."

Horrible hairy hogs hurrying homeward on heavily harnessed horses

BOOK TITLE
Animalia
AUTHOR
Graeme Base
ILLUSTRATOR
Graeme Base
PUBLISHER
Penguin Books Australia Ltd.
Harry N. Abrams, New York
PUBLICATION DATE
1987
ILLUSTRATION MEDIUM
Inks, gouache and pencil

"Animalia *came from a great love of animals and a desire to create a book with huge amounts of detail and things to discover. That was the sort of book I remember enjoying as a child. I concealed the figure of a little boy in every picture at the last minute in an attempt to link all the pictures together somehow.* Animalia *took three years to produce, largely because I was working in a new style and had to experiment as I went along.*"

Nicola Bayley

Nicola Bayley was born in Singapore in 1949. She was educated at a convent school and studied art at St. Martin's and the Royal College of Art. She has a distinctive style, producing detailed, brilliantly colored miniature illustrations, and has been described as "the most gifted and talented naturalistic illustrator working in Britain today." Her first published work was *Nicola Bayley's Book of Nursery Rhymes* (1975), and since its success she has illustrated numerous picture books. *The Mousehole Cat* won the Illustrated Children's Book of the Year, 1990, awarded by *Publishing News*.

BOOK TITLE
The Mousehole Cat
AUTHOR
Antonia Barber
ILLUSTRATOR
Nicola Bayley
PUBLISHER
Walker Books Ltd., London
Macmillan Publishing Co.
New York
PUBLICATION DATE
1990
ILLUSTRATION MEDIUM
Watercolor

Quentin Blake

Quentin Blake was born in 1932. He started drawing for the magazine *Punch* while still at school and read English at Downing College, Cambridge, before becoming a freelance illustrator. He has illustrated nearly one hundred books for children and several for adults. In 1965 he became a part-time tutor at the Royal College of Art where from 1978–1986 he was head of the Illustration Department and is now a Visiting Professor. He was made an RDI (Royal Designer for Industry) in 1981, and an OBE (Officer Order of the British Empire) in the New Year's Honors List in 1988.

BOOK TITLE
Quentin Blake's ABC
AUTHOR
Quentin Blake
ILLUSTRATOR
Quentin Blake
PUBLISHER
Jonathan Cape, London
Alfred A. Knopf, New York
PUBLICATION DATE
1989
ILLUSTRATION MEDIUM
India ink and watercolor

BOOK TITLE
Mrs. Armitage on Wheels
AUTHOR
Quentin Blake
ILLUSTRATOR
Quentin Blake
PUBLISHER
Jonathan Cape, London
Alfred A. Knopf Inc., New York
PUBLICATION DATE
1987
ILLUSTRATION MEDIUM
India ink and watercolor

BOOK TITLE
Mister Magnolia
AUTHOR
Quentin Blake
ILLUSTRATOR
Quentin Blake
PUBLISHER
Jonathan Cape, London
PUBLICATION DATE
1980
ILLUSTRATION MEDIUM
India ink, watercolor and
watercolor pastel

"One area of interest common to Mrs. Armitage on Wheels *and* Mister Magnolia *is that of orchestrating the narrative so that the reader wants to go on turning the pages to find out what happens: so that although the drawings have an air of spontaneity, the design and sequence of the pages is very carefully planned in advance. A fluid method of coloring adds to the pen line without interfering with it, and contributes (I hope) to a sense of movement."*

Jan Brett

BOOK TITLE
The Owl and the Pussycat
AUTHOR
Edward Lear
ILLUSTRATOR
Jan Brett
PUBLISHER
G.P. Putnam's Sons
PUBLICATION DATE
1991
ILLUSTRATION MEDIUM
Watercolor

Jan Brett decided to be an illustrator at an early age and spent many hours reading and drawing throughout her childhood. While a student at the Boston Museum School she often visited the Museum of Fine Arts, and today she is delighted and surprised when fragments of the beautiful images she saw there come back to her in her painting. Together with her husband, who is a member of the Boston Symphony Orchestra, Ms. Brett travels extensively, visiting many countries of the world where she researches the costumes and architecture that appear in her work. Her highly acclaimed books have appeared on the Top Ten Bestseller Lists in *Publishers Weekly, The New York Times,* and *Parents* magazine, as well as many others. Her artwork has been exhibited in galleries and museums throughout the United States.

"I visited the Caribbean island of Martinique to find ideas for the setting of The Owl and the Pussycat. *It was just the place to sail away for a year and a day. I sketched the flowers that appear on each page, I studied traditional dresses made of Madras, and I marveled at the colorful fish under the water. Being there gave me so many ideas I needed to add an underwater border to fit everything in."*

BOOK TITLE
The Mitten
AUTHOR
Jan Brett
ILLUSTRATOR
Jan Brett
PUBLISHER
G.P. Putnam's Sons
PUBLICATION DATE
1989
ILLUSTRATION MEDIUM
Watercolor

"*I love to fall asleep knowing the world outside is bare and brown, and then to wake up to a new snowfall that transforms everything into a magical place. That is why I love to draw snowy scenes. I can imagine anything happening.*"

"*In* The Mitten, *Nicki explores the snowy woods in the borders. I thought that as each animal rushed out into the snow they would want to get into the cozy mitten. I wasn't sure how they would get out until I imagined how the bear felt when the mouse found a spot on his tender nose. Just thinking about how his nose would feel gave me the answer.*"

BOOK TITLE
The Wild Christmas Reindeer
AUTHOR
Jan Brett
ILLUSTRATOR
Jan Brett
PUBLISHER
G.P. Putnam's Sons
PUBLICATION DATE
1990
ILLUSTRATION MEDIUM
Watercolor

"*I noticed that when I rode my horse, Westy, that he became frantic and wild if I was rough or too bossy. If I used a gentle voice and was patient, he was a good boy. I thought that Santa Claus could ask a little elf girl to get the reindeer ready for Christmas, and the very same thing could happen to her.*"

"*I always imagined the North Pole would look just like the way I drew it in the book. I like to find each one of the border towers in the big picture of Santa's Winterfarm.*"

Patience Brewster

Photo: Julia Miller

BOOK TITLE
Rabbit Inn
AUTHOR
Patience Brewster
ILLUSTRATOR
Patience Brewster
PUBLISHER
Little, Brown and Co.
PUBLICATION DATE
1991
ILLUSTRATION MEDIUM
Watercolor inks, paint, pencil

Patience Brewster earned her B.F.A. in printmaking and bookmaking at the Philadelphia College of Art. She has illustrated 17 books, three of which she authored. *Bear and Mrs. Duck* was nominated for the 1991 Golden Sower Award and was also selected as an ALA *Booklist* Children's Editors' Choice. Patience Brewster's illustrations have been exhibited in one-woman shows in Nantucket, Massachusetts, New York City and Ithaca, New York. In addition, she has designed posters for the Syracuse Opera Company and for the "Original Art Show" in NYC. She resides in Skaneateles, New York, with her husband and two children.

"If you need an example of an illustrator completely enjoying her/himself…this is it! I had the characters in this book milling around in my mind for 13 years, when they gathered together and got in the Rabbit Inn. They were ready and I was ready! I felt I could move these characters into any activity or arena and dress them up in anything I wished. This was truly my experience of unlimited joy. I used my pets, my favorite colors, the garden I wish I had, the fabrics I wish I could find, and let all the characters do whatever they could think of, as long as it went with the text to a reasonable degree."

BOOK TITLE
Bear and Mrs. Duck
AUTHOR
Elizabeth Winthrop
ILLUSTRATOR
Patience Brewster
PUBLISHER
Holiday House
PUBLICATION DATE
1988
ILLUSTRATION MEDIUM
Watercolor dyes and pencil

BOOK TITLE
**Princess Abigail & the Wonderful
Hat**
AUTHOR
Steven Kroll
ILLUSTRATOR
Patience Brewster
PUBLISHER
Holiday House
PUBLICATION DATE
1991
ILLUSTRATION MEDIUM
Watercolor, ink and pencil

"When I was illustrating Bear and Mrs. Duck *I was in the process of moving into and fixing up a 'new' very old house. I carried a lot of this process into this book. I tried the colors of my walls out on the walls in the book. If I liked them they went in the book and in the house! I had become intimate with the mouldings and windows of the house and so they also appeared in the book. I had no problem with executing the emotions in the story because my life's work had been trying to break in babysitters. I loved creating the perfect one. But, it wasn't until the hat went on her head, that Mrs. Duck became who she is today."*

"It was so exciting, after ten years of <u>asking</u> to finally get a fairy tale. I loved having a princess to draw and I loved creating a green, wrinkley, friendly-giant-lizard. The fairy tale is not purely traditional, so I carried over the fanciful modern twist on romantic history into my characters and colors. This was set in fall. My palette is usually lighter and paler. So I gathered huge baskets of fall <u>in fall</u> and made myself a 'hat of nature' like the one in the story, to fill my studio with purples and golds and rich browns and dark rose wines, since I would be illustrating this fall book in spring and summer!"

"The page describing horrid, bow-legged, buck-teethed, sneary, piggy, flabby Prince Grindstone was definitely the most challenging…Just read the description and imagine what you would draw!"

Eric Carle

BOOK TITLE
The Very Hungry Caterpillar
AUTHOR
Eric Carle
ILLUSTRATOR
Eric Carle
PUBLISHER
Philomel Books
PUBLICATION DATE
1969
ILLUSTRATION MEDIUM
Collage

Born to German immigrant parents in Syracuse, New York, Eric Carle remembers childhood walks through meadows and woods with his father, an experience which shaped his appreciation of nature and his fascination with the animal world. In 1935 his family returned to Germany, settling in Stuttgart where Eric later studied graphic design at the Akademie der Bildenden Künste. He returned to New York in 1952, working as a commercial artist until the mid-1960s when he illustrated his first children's book. He subsequently wrote *The Very Hungry Caterpillar* which garnered awards in England, France, Japan and the U.S. where it was named a *New York Times* Best Illustrated Children's Book in 1969. Today, Eric Carle's books are published around the world in 17 languages.

BOOK TITLE
Eric Carle's Animals, Animals
AUTHOR
Compiled by Laura Whipple
ILLUSTRATOR
Eric Carle
PUBLISHER
Philomel Books
PUBLICATION DATE
1989
ILLUSTRATION MEDIUM
Collage

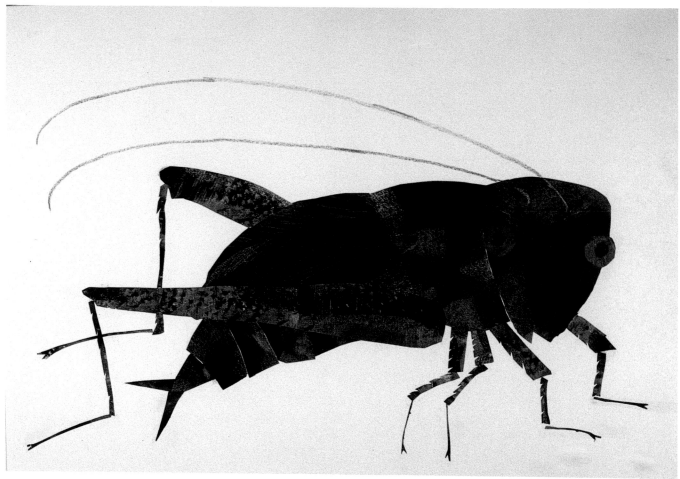

BOOK TITLE
The Very Quiet Cricket
AUTHOR
Eric Carle
ILLUSTRATOR
Eric Carle
PUBLISHER
Philomel Books
PUBLICATION DATE
1990
ILLUSTRATION MEDIUM
Collage

Peter Catalanotto

BOOK TITLE
Dylan's Day Out
AUTHOR
Peter Catalanotto
ILLUSTRATOR
Peter Catalanotto
PUBLISHER
Orchard Books
PUBLICATION DATE
1989
ILLUSTRATION MEDIUM
Watercolor

Peter Catalanotto graduated from Pratt Institute in 1981 and started working as a freelance illustrator for such publications as *Reader's Digest, Family Circle* and *Woman's Day.* He has painted over 150 young adult book jackets. After entering the children's book field in 1988, he was named Most Promising New Artist in a *Publisher's Weekly* poll of booksellers in 1990. His original artwork has been shown at the Elizabeth Stone Gallery in Birmingham, Michigan.

"*I* started my illustration career doing a lot of black-and-white paintings for newspapers. I wanted to use B/W somehow in my first book. The challenge was coming up with enough B/W characters and items for a story, then to make them all flow throughout the book. I wanted B/W to be the theme without forcing the issue."

"Being a dog owner and a high school soccer player the story came naturally. The book has very few words, allowing the viewer to follow and interpret the off-beat occurrences from many different angles and perspectives."

BOOK TITLE
Mr. Mumble
AUTHOR
Peter Catalanotto
ILLUSTRATOR
Peter Catalanotto
PUBLISHER
Orchard Books
PUBLICATION DATE
1990
ILLUSTRATION MEDIUM
Watercolor

"*Since I've spent my life mumbling and drawing I wanted to create a book about being misunderstood. I spent months coming up with the right jokes or 'mumbles.' They not only had to be funny verbally but, more important, visually.*"

"*It's amazing how much time and work go into something to make it look like it came off the top of your head. Like Dylan's Day Out I tried to keep the reader off balance by constantly changing perspectives. Entering a different world should be viewed a different way.*"

"*I wanted to create a sweet, charming man who is everbody's grand-father or uncle.*"

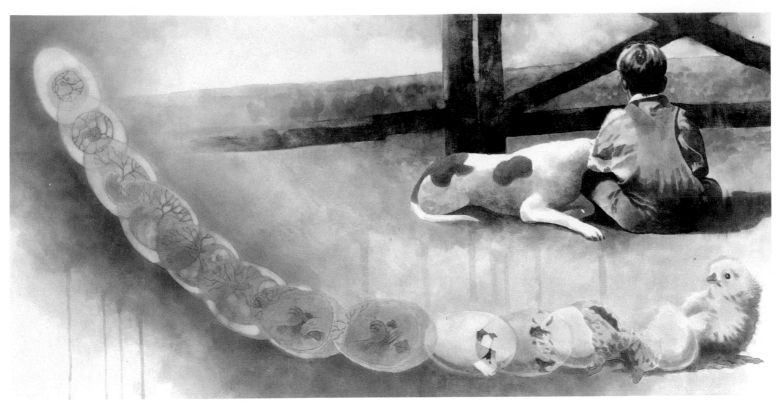

"*George Ella Lyon created a very powerful yet very simple, subtle text. I wanted my imagery to reflect this. That's why I took common objects like an egg or a chair to evoke strong emotions.*"

"*A challenge was to show strong emotions and occurrences like hope, fear and war in quiet tones. Watercolor allowed me to keep the imagery soft and lingering. Creating beautiful paintings isn't enough. An illustrator has to enhance the writer's text, adding new dimensions to the story.*"

BOOK TITLE
Cecil's Story
AUTHOR
George Ella Lyon
ILLUSTRATOR
Peter Catalanotto
PUBLISHER
Orchard Books
PUBLICATION DATE
1991
ILLUSTRATION MEDIUM
Watercolor

Chris Conover

"I was born and raised in New York City. My parents were fine artists, both of whom had their work in major collections. I was lucky to grow up with art all around me. I attended New York's famous High School of Music and Art, and went on to the State University of New York at Buffalo, where I studied fine art and printmaking. My career in children's book illustration represents the realization of a lifelong dream, stemming from my strong attachment to favorite books as a child. I have been illustrating books since 1974—seventeen in all. *Six Little Ducks* was a *Boston Globe-Horn Book* Honor Book and *Froggie Went A-Courting* was chosen as a Metropolitan Museum Christmas Book. Three of my books won American Institute of Graphic Arts citations. My original illustrations are in several well-known collections, including the Aga Khan family, Cranbrook School, Lilly Library, and the Mazza Collection at Findlay Library."

" 'Froggie Went A-Courting' *is a rhyme that always made me smile, and I enjoyed retelling it. There are already hundreds of versions of it so I felt pretty free about eliminating the gobbling of the characters by a marauding cat and substituting a comic ending."*

"I think that an engaging main character is terrifically important, and the character of Froggie was pure fun to create and share. I would think 'How would Froggie handle this situation?' (charming Miss Mouse, winning over Uncle Rat, dancing at his wedding) and then do sketch after sketch until I had one with the requisite panache. After finishing this book, I felt quite sad to no longer have this character to draw—he had become a pal!"

BOOK TITLE
Froggie Went A-Courting
AUTHOR
Retold by Chris Conover
ILLUSTRATOR
Chris Conover
PUBLISHER
Farrar, Straus & Giroux
PUBLICATION DATE
1986
ILLUSTRATION MEDIUM
Watercolor with pen and ink

BOOK TITLE
Mother Goose and the Sly Fox
AUTHOR
Chris Conover
ILLUSTRATOR
Chris Conover
PUBLISHER
Farrar, Straus & Giroux
PUBLICATION DATE
1989
ILLUSTRATION MEDIUM
Watercolor, ink line

"*This is a very special story, with a reassuring message that is important for children to hear. I concentrated on storytelling, both visual and verbal, even in my choice of palette. I used primarily warm, earthy tones to echo the Goose's motherly warmth. I chose detail with an eye to expressing the characters' personalities more eloquently. For example: Mother Goose's 'baby picture'—a basket of eggs—hanging in her workplace.*"

"*Just before beginning work on this book, I took a wonderful trip to Holland and visited the little town where my family came from. This gave me a rich sense of time and place and had a very strong effect on the design of the book.*"

BOOK TITLE
Six Little Ducks
AUTHOR
Retold by Chris Conover
ILLUSTRATOR
Chris Conover
PUBLISHER
Thomas Y. Crowell
PUBLICATION DATE
1976
ILLUSTRATION MEDIUM
Watercolor with black line overlay

"*Six Little Ducks was my very first book. Challenging? Was it ever!*"

"*The text is an activity song that I learned while working as a day camp counselor. It was evident that children loved the song, they sang it daily. Therefore, it seemed a perfect idea, and I set about weaving a visual narrative into the verse to enrich the simple text. I was very eager to illustrate a children's book and plunged into this project without the benefit of formal training as an illustrator. My enthusiasm came in handy, too, because I completed two sets of illustrations for this book in order that it be published.*"

Barbara Cooney

Photo: © Janet Knott, Boston Globe

BOOK TITLE
Ox-Cart Man
AUTHOR
Donald Hall
ILLUSTRATOR
Barbara Cooney
PUBLISHER
Viking Penguin
PUBLICATION DATE
1979
ILLUSTRATION MEDIUM
Acrylic (a wash of sepia across the boards as a base to simulate the wood panels that itinerant painters of that day used)

Barbara Cooney was born in Room 1127 of the Hotel Brossert in Brooklyn, New York. After growing up on Long Island, she studied art and art history at Smith College and later took courses at the Art Students League in New York City. She has illustrated over 100 books for children. Graceful charm, intelligent use of color, meticulous research, and attention to detail are the hallmarks of her work. Among her many awards are two Caldecott Medals for *Chanticleer and the Fox* and *Ox-Cart Man,* as well as the National Book Award for *Miss Rumphius.* She has received numerous honorary doctorates and in 1976 was awarded the Smith College Medal.

*"*Ox-Cart Man *was a 'natural' in that the country of the Ox-Cart* Man *was my countryside too, albeit I was living just across the state line in Massachusetts. I lived in an old old house with an identical kitchen. The main challenge was to pick a date when this story could have happened and then be sure all props, costumes, etc., were authentic. The date I came up with was 1832. I wanted to bring that period to life, to show country living exactly as it was in New England in 1832."*

BOOK TITLE
Roxaboxen
AUTHOR
Alice McLerran
ILLUSTRATOR
Barbara Cooney
PUBLISHER
Lothrop, Lee & Shepard
PUBLICATION DATE
1991
ILLUSTRATION MEDIUM
**Acrylic and pastel because of the
brilliancy and huge range of
earth colors provided by pastels**

"*Being a green-grass and green-leaves person, I saw* Roxaboxen *as one of my toughest assignments: constructing a magical world out of something that wasn't there. I made two trips to the desert, where I found a small tan hill dotted with stones and rocks, a scattering of desert plants, and now lots of broken glass and an old car chassis. But accompanied by Alice McLerran's eighty-year-old Aunt Frances (former Roxaboxenite), the magic and spirit of* Roxaboxen *began to emerge. The desert was for me an acquired—and lasting—taste. Its changing magic is what I hoped to evoke.*"

BOOK TITLE
Miss Rumphius
AUTHOR
Barbara Cooney
ILLUSTRATOR
Barbara Cooney
PUBLISHER
Viking Penguin
PUBLICATION DATE
1982
ILLUSTRATION MEDIUM
**Acrylic on gesso-coated percale—
a painterly, gentle technique for a
thoughtful story**

"*This book was written in the form of a modern fairy tale. It was based on the fact that a neighbor in Maine each summer collected lupine seeds and threw them about. A pretty thought. One day I sat down and started my fairy story. I was definitely not preaching a lesson—just making another story where things happened in threes. The bulk of the story is biographical (family happenings)—also autobiographical, since it follows the course of my life (except for the lupine seeds idea).*"

Donald Crews

A graduate of Cooper Union, Don Crews worked as a designer and assistant magazine art director before pursuing a career in freelance design with his wife, Ann Jonas. He published his first children's book in 1967 and since then has garnered numerous awards. Both *Freight Train* and *Truck* were Caldecott Honor Books; *Flying* was named a *New York Times* Best Illustrated Children's Book of the Year; and *Carousel* was an ALA Notable book. Mr. Crews' work is in the permanent exhibit at the Mazza Collection at Findlay College and was shown at the Henry Feiwel Gallery and in Japan in a 1990 exhibition titled "Picture Books Edited by Susan Hirschman."

BOOK TITLE
Carousel
AUTHOR
Donald Crews
ILLUSTRATOR
Donald Crews
PUBLISHER
Greenwillow Books
PUBLICATION DATE
1982
ILLUSTRATION MEDIUM
Gouache paintings and 35mm Kodachrome transparencies

"*I* don't think there is an activity more identified with fun and children than a ride on a carousel. Having overcome my reluctance to introduce figurative representation in my stories with Parade, a carousel ride became a possibility."

"A carousel ride, a moving carousel, a musical carousel were absolute requirements. Getting a carousel to go was my challenge. Investigation on various ways of achieving this movement were unconvincing. Some experiments were interesting but not usable. Photography, one of my methods of gathering visual information (sketching), revealed the solution."

"I created my carousel and photographed my painting, moving the camera at various speeds and directions before the shutter clicked shut. Several rolls of color film later, I was able to select a series of images that best represented a carousel ride. The 'sound' was created in the same manner."

"My mail from my young audience often notes that, Carousel, while a lot of fun, makes them sick. I guess it works."

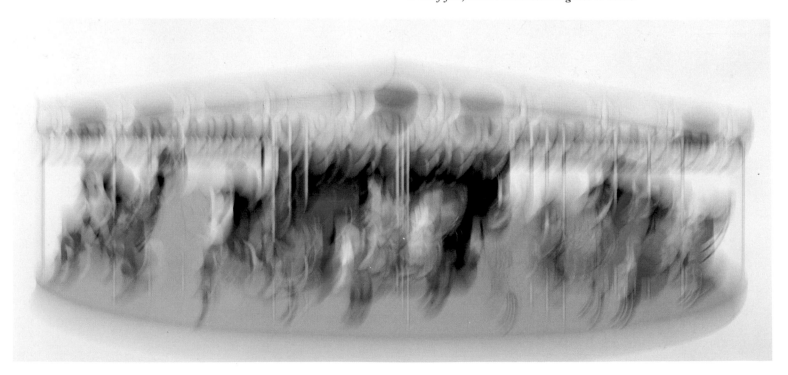

BOOK TITLE
Truck
AUTHOR
Donald Crews
ILLUSTRATOR
Donald Crews
PUBLISHER
Greenwillow Books
PUBLICATION DATE
1980
ILLUSTRATION MEDIUM
Pre-separated art

"Identifying and somehow capturing the spirit of a subject or event is central to my approach to a story. The power, scale and motion of trucks was the story I wanted to tell."

"Using images that filled the spreads, details of images and cropping to further exaggerate the size of these vehicles give my Truck *its character. Eliminating figures helps to keep the reader focused on just who the star is."*

"A bright red truck makes it easy to follow as the pages are turned. The scale is reduced from page to page. Then at the end the truck comes back to the size from which it started, completing the cycle."

"Keeping the book wordless, but for the signs along the way, and on the trucks, allows one to move unimpeded to the end."

BOOK TITLE
Flying
AUTHOR
Donald Crews
ILLUSTRATOR
Donald Crews
PUBLISHER
Greenwillow Books
PUBLICATION DATE
1986
ILLUSTRATION MEDIUM
**Gouache and airbrush
reflective art**

"*Flying was the missing means of getting from here to there in my stories. I wanted my book to capture the hypnotic feeling of a plane trip. I chose a commuter plane because it flies closer to the ground and makes the identifiable objects believable. The landscape is abstracted and selectively detailed to emphasize the distance between it and the plane.*"

"*The text is simple and repetitive to accentuate the lolling mood of a plane ride. The plane on the page changes direction from spread to spread, the way a plane does in actuality. The typography gets airborne when the plane does and comes down again with it at the end.*"

"*The excitement of taking off, the awe of the changing landscape and the relief at landing was where I wanted my readers to be.*"

BOOK TITLE
Freight Train
AUTHOR
Donald Crews
ILLUSTRATOR
Donald Crews
PUBLISHER
Greenwillow Books
PUBLICATION DATE
1979
ILLUSTRATION MEDIUM
Airbrush/pre-separated art

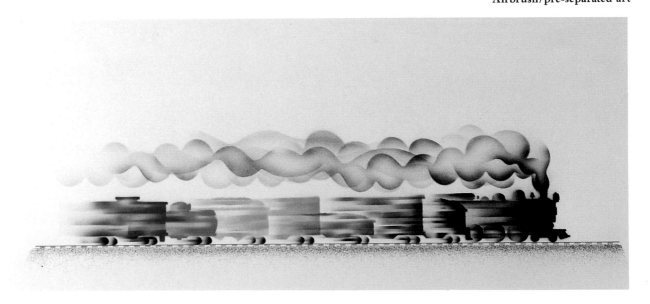

"*I assume that almost everyone is as excited as I am about trains. Trains in real life, toy trains, train sounds, train stories. I hoped my paean to trains would be able to convey some of that excitement, the magic of a train moving across the landscape. I watched steam locomotives pulling freights from my grandmother's farm in Florida, and they impressed me greatly.*"

"*Years later their graphic qualities made them perfect subject material. I chose an airbrush as the tool to set my train in motion. The ability to shade color and soften edges (focus) is very important to the motion.*"

Pat Cummings

BOOK TITLE
Storm in the Night
AUTHOR
Mary Stolz
ILLUSTRATOR
Pat Cummings
PUBLISHER
HarperCollins
PUBLICATION DATE
1988
ILLUSTRATION MEDIUM
Acrylic

Pat Cummings graduated from Pratt Institute with a B.F.A. in communications design. Growing up in an army base family that moved every two or three years, she found that art was a way of getting involved in the many schools she attended. Living in foreign countries generated her love for fantasy and a nomadic childhood gave her a closeness with her family that is reflected in her books. A Visiting Distinguished Professor at Queens College, New York, Ms. Cummings teaches creative writing for picture books. In addition to the Coretta Scott King award for *My Mama Needs Me*, she has received Coretta Scott King Honor Book Awards for *Storm in the Night*, *C.L.O.U.D.S.* and *Just Us Women*.

"The text of the story, with its rich imagery, was a challenge. Since the action takes place during a rainy night, I wanted to illuminate scenes with the colors of lightning flashes or woodburning stoves. By using acrylic paint, I knew I could start with a dark background and bring out the highlights, almost the reverse of my normal approach. I wanted the reader to sense what I did when reading the text: the smells and sounds of a rainy southern night, and the closeness of the grandfather and child wrapped up in the darkness."

BOOK TITLE
C.L.O.U.D.S.
AUTHOR
Pat Cummings
ILLUSTRATOR
Pat Cummings
PUBLISHER
Lothrop, Lee & Shepard
PUBLICATION DATE
1986
ILLUSTRATION MEDIUM
Watercolor, airbrush, pencil

"Doing C.L.O.U.D.S. required inventing an entire fantasy environment for the main character, Chuku. I thought that using an airbrush to paint the skyscapes he inhabits would give me the smooth tones and gradations of colors that I wanted. As a long term cloud-watcher myself, I hoped that readers would be inspired to see the sky as the continually changing artistic creation that I tried to capture in the book."

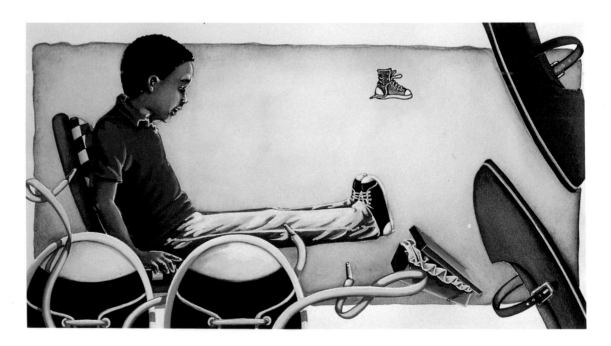

BOOK TITLE
I Need a Lunch Box
AUTHOR
Jeanette Caines
ILLUSTRATOR
Pat Cummings
PUBLISHER
HarperCollins
PUBLICATION DATE
1988
ILLUSTRATION MEDIUM
Watercolor and rubber stamps

"There are very few lines of text in this story, so I knew that I wanted the art to supply a lot of details about the characters. I decided to use watercolors and rubber stamps because the story had a lot of whimsy to it: the little boy fantasizes about all the possible lunch boxes that he could fill. I wanted to show, with all of the patterns and colors and objects, the richness and surprises of the boy's imagination."

Tomie dePaola

BOOK TITLE
Tomie dePaola's Mother Goose
COMPILER
Tomie dePaola
ILLUSTRATOR
Tomie dePaola

PUBLISHER
G.P. Putnam's Sons
PUBLICATION DATE
1985
ILLUSTRATION MEDIUM
Rotring Artist Color on 140 lb. Fabriano Artistico hand-made paper

Photo: Jon Gilbert Fox

Since graduating from Pratt Institute in 1956, Tomie dePaola has been a professional artist and designer, teacher of art, painter and muralist, and artist and author of children's books. He has illustrated almost 200 books, many of which he has also written. His major recognitions include a Caldecott Honor Award for *Strega Nona* in 1976, The Kerlan Award in recognition of singular attainments in the creations of children's literature, 1981, the Regina Medal, 1983, the Smithson Award, 1990, and a U.S. nomination for the Hans Christian Andersen Medal in 1990. Published in more than 15 countries, over five million of his books are in print. Mr. dePaola has also designed greeting cards, posters, magazine and catalog covers, record album covers, and theater and nightclub sets. His work has been widely exhibited, is housed in the Kerlan Collection at the University of Minnesota, the Osborne Collection in Toronto, and is found in private collections worldwide.

Tomie dePaola received an M.F.A. at The California College of Arts and Crafts, Oakland, and earned doctoral equivalency at Lone Mountain College, San Francisco.

"In illustrating a great classic, such as Mother Goose, the challenge is to find a new way of looking at old friends. My art director, Nanette Stevenson, and I plotted out the book and determined that I should try to keep an open design, clear color, and an overall joyousness. I used a dark brown line to delineate the stylized figures and settings concentrating on simple shapes and clarity of composition."

BOOK TITLE
Tony's Bread
AUTHOR
Tomie dePaola
ILLUSTRATOR
Tomie dePaola
PUBLISHER
G.P. Putnam's Sons
PUBLICATION DATE
1989
ILLUSTRATION MEDIUM
**Rotring Artists Color on 140 lb.
Fabriano Artistico
hand-made paper**

"*I can say that in* Tony's Bread *I used what is called 'a typical dePaola style.' I suppose this means rounded figures, humorous expressions, and clear vibrant colors. I love doing humorous books and, of course, when I write the story myself, I have a certain control over the images as well. The three 'zie'—aunts—were fun. I saw them joined at the hip creating one huge black shape with hands and faces peering out. You need only to go to an Italian village to see they are not a figment of my imagination.*"

BOOK TITLE
The Legend of the Bluebonnet
AUTHOR
Tomie dePaola
ILLUSTRATOR
Tomie dePaola
PUBLISHER
G.P. Putnam's Sons
PUBLICATION DATE
1983
ILLUSTRATION MEDIUM
**Transparent colored inks,
tempera, and watercolor on
Fabriano 140 lb. hand-made
watercolor paper**

"*Since my first trip to the Southwest, I had always been interested in doing a book concerning Native Americans utilizing Native American artifacts and design. I tried to capture the bleakness of the Texas prairies in drought and then contrasting this with deep blue night skies, brilliant fire, and, of course, the spectacular beauty of the bluebonnet flower itself. I used more modelling and even though I stylized, I tried to give She-Who-Is-Alone an extremely human face.*"

Henrik Drescher

Born in Denmark, Henrik Drescher spent his childhood in Copenhagen and came to the U.S. in his early teens. As a child he would look through books, searching for clues about how they came to be. Today, he enjoys making books by hand. Perhaps best known for *Simon's Book*—a Reading Rainbow feature selection, *Parents' Choice* Award for Book Illustration and a winner of *The New York Times* Best Illustrated Children's Book Award in 1983—Mr. Drescher has also won acclaim for *The Strange Appearance of Howard Cranebill, Jr.,* and *Looking for Santa Claus.*

BOOK TITLE
Simon's Book
AUTHOR
Henrik Drescher
ILLUSTRATOR
Henrik Drescher
PUBLISHER
Lothrop, Lee & Shepard
PUBLICATION DATE
1983
ILLUSTRATION MEDIUM
Collage, watercolor, ink

He looked like Santa Claus, but his name was Igor.

BOOK TITLE
Looking for Santa Claus
AUTHOR
Henrik Drescher
ILLUSTRATOR
Henrik Drescher
PUBLISHER
Lothrop, Lee & Shepard
PUBLICATION DATE
1984
ILLUSTRATION MEDIUM
Collage, watercolor, ink

"My books grow out of visual concepts. I 'build' the book as a picture book and apply the words last. I use whatever materials I need to express my ideas."

BOOK TITLE
**The Strange Appearance of
Howard Cranebill, Jr.**
AUTHOR
Henrik Drescher
ILLUSTRATOR
Henrik Drescher
PUBLISHER
Lothrop, Lee & Shepard
PUBLICATION DATE
1982
ILLUSTRATION MEDIUM
Collage, watercolor, ink

Richard Egielski

"In The Tub People almost the entire story takes place in a bathtub. The most challenging aspect of this book was doing 16 pictures that have the bathtub as a backdrop and making each picture interesting and different."

"I began my art training at the High School of Art and Design in New York City. From there I went on to Pratt Institute and Parsons School of Design where I studied with Maurice Sendak. My first published picture book was *Sid & Sol,* written by Arthur Yorinks, published in 1977. Since then Arthur and I have collaborated on eight picture books, including *Hey, Al* which won the 1987 Caldecott Medal."

BOOK TITLE
The Tub People
AUTHOR
Pam Conrad
ILLUSTRATOR
Richard Egielski
PUBLISHER
HarperCollins
PUBLICATION DATE
1989
ILLUSTRATION MEDIUM
Watercolor

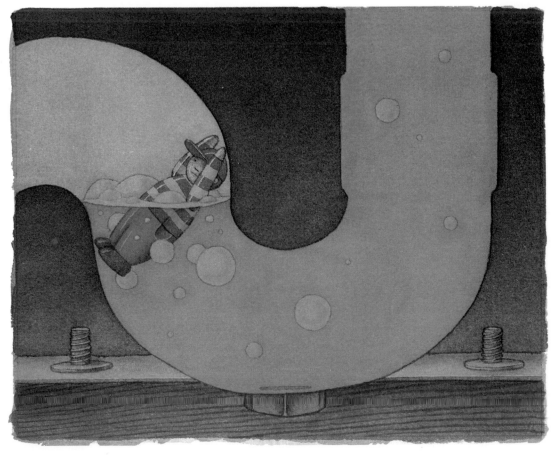

BOOK TITLE
Hey, Al
AUTHOR
Arthur Yorinks
ILLUSTRATOR
Richard Egielski
PUBLISHER
Farrar, Straus & Giroux
PUBLICATION DATE
1986
ILLUSTRATION MEDIUM
Watercolor

"*Movies, especially those that I saw as a child, are a continuing influence on my work. Bird Island in Hey, Al is based on King Kong's Skull Island.*"

BOOK TITLE
Oh, Brother
AUTHOR
Arthur Yorinks
ILLUSTRATOR
Richard Egielski
PUBLISHER
Farrar, Straus & Giroux
PUBLICATION DATE
1989
ILLUSTRATION MEDIUM
Watercolor

"*Oh, Brother is the largest (9″ × 12″) and longest (40 pages) picture book that I have ever done. So the pictures were bigger than usual and there were a lot more of them.*"

"*The story begins: 'It was a sorry accident at sea many years ago that...' The author doesn't say what the accident was, so I particularly enjoyed inventing and pictorially telling the incident of the twins fighting over a rocket and knocking a lantern into a box of fireworks, thus blowing up the ship.*"

Lois Ehlert

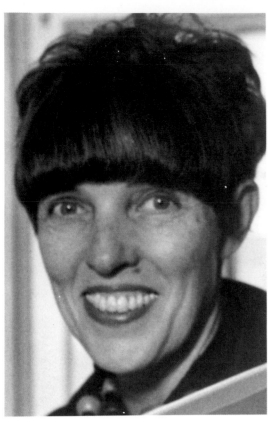

BOOK TITLE
Color Zoo
AUTHOR
Lois Ehlert
ILLUSTRATOR
Lois Ehlert
PUBLISHER
J.B. Lippincott
PUBLICATION DATE
1989
ILLUSTRATION MEDIUM
Cut paper/collage

Lois Ehlert graduated from Layton School of Art, Milwaukee, and continued post-graduate studies at the University of Wisconsin/Milwaukee. She works as a freelance graphic designer and illustrator, illustrating both trade and textbooks for children. She also teaches children's art classes. Her work has received recognition from the Society of Illustrators, New York Art Directors, *Print Annual, Graphis Annual,* Art Museum Association of America, Wisconsin Arts Board, American Institute of Graphic Arts, and most recently the Caldecott Honor Award for *Color Zoo.* Although she has illustrated many children's books, it is only recently that she has begun to combine art and text, using her graphic design skills to form the complete book.

"Having spent many years teaching art to children, I wanted to do a concept book of shapes and colors, but not one in which the child would learn to draw by copying my forms. I began with some experiments with apertures, and spent about two years making it look so simple. The book is actually a slow form of animation. The book ends with a reiteration of shapes and colors."

ARTICHOKE
artichoke

AVOCADO avocado

APPLE
apple

ASPARAGUS asparagus

APRICOT apricot

BOOK TITLE
Eating the Alphabet
AUTHOR
Lois Ehlert
ILLUSTRATOR
Lois Ehlert
PUBLISHER
Harcourt Brace Jovanovich
PUBLICATION DATE
1989
ILLUSTRATION MEDIUM
Watercolor collage

"*Using a combination of common and exotic fruits and vegetables, I gradually ate and painted my way through the alphabet. The watercolor/collages enabled me to present visual information so a child could recognize unfamiliar fruits and vegetables. Note that identification labels are capital letters as well as lowercase. The information found during research was so interesting, it was decided to include a glossary.*"

His food in a can
is tame and mild,

BOOK TITLE
Feathers for Lunch
AUTHOR
Lois Ehlert
ILLUSTRATOR
Lois Ehlert
PUBLISHER
Harcourt Brace Jovanovich
PUBLICATION DATE
1990
ILLUSTRATION MEDIUM
Watercolor collage

"*This book is designed to be used for a variety of ages. It is an introduction to common birds. The birds are actual size, the coloration correct but not complex. Watercolor/collages show the beautiful subtleties of the birds and late spring flowers. Large type carries the story line, small black type identifies objects, small red type indicates sound. The typography is very integrated into the page design.*"

Chicka chicka...
BOOM! BOOM!

BOOK TITLE
Chicka Chicka Boom Boom
AUTHOR
**Bill Martin, Jr. and
John Archambault**
ILLUSTRATOR
Lois Ehlert
PUBLISHER
Simon & Schuster
PUBLICATION DATE
1989
ILLUSTRATION MEDIUM
Cut paper/collage

"*The text of this book presented some very abstract concepts for me to illustrate. Illustrating a letter of the alphabet climbing up the trunk of a coconut tree seemed impossible until I read the verse several times, enjoying its rhythms. I decided to dispense with reality and illustrate it as a piece of music. The art is made of cut, painted paper.*"

I'd flip down rivers and splash in the sea.

BOOK TITLE
Fish Eyes
AUTHOR
Lois Ehlert
ILLUSTRATOR
Lois Ehlert
PUBLISHER
Harcourt Brace Jovanovich
PUBLICATION DATE
1990
ILLUSTRATION MEDIUM
Cut paper/collage

"*This is a counting book, presenting fish, such as 'three smiling fish,' in which eyes of each fish are die-cut circles. A young child can count by placing a finger in each hole. There is a minor text printed black on blue, plus a dark minnow that swims through the book making comments. I am happy when I can use pure, flat colors, making the fish move and flip with color vibrations. Note that the book is fish-size.*"

Leonard Everett Fisher

BOOK TITLE
The ABC Exhibit
AUTHOR
Leonard Everett Fisher
ILLUSTRATOR
Leonard Everett Fisher
PUBLISHER
Macmillan Publishing Co.
PUBLICATION DATE
1991
ILLUSTRATION MEDIUM
Acrylic

Leonard Everett Fisher has illustrated 240 books for young readers since 1955, writing about 65 of these. A graduate of Yale University and recipient of its Winchester Fellowship, Mr. Fisher holds the 1991 Regina Medal of the Catholic Library Association; the 1991 Kerlan Award of the University of Minnesota; and the 1989 *Washington Post* Children's Book Guild Nonfiction Award, among many others. His art and papers are included in the collections of the Library of Congress, Smithsonian Institution, New Britain Museum, as well as numerous other museums and universities. In 1979 he was a delegate-at-large to the White House Conference on Library and Information Services, and he is past president of the Westport, Connecticut, Public Library. Mr. Fisher has designed a number of U.S. postage stamps including the Bicentennial issues of 1972 and 1977, and the commemorative *The Legend of Sleepy Hollow.*

"*The intent here was not to create a thematic ABC but to offer straightforward images (i.e., paintings) that were letter-connected and not too far removed from a young reader's reach and understanding. The whole of this giving the impression that the reader or viewer was passing through a picture gallery or exhibition — the book itself being the gallery and the exhibition catalog as well. It is an attempt to instruct in the language of artistic vision rather than designed objects.*"

BOOK TITLE
Space Songs
AUTHOR
Myra Cohn Livingston
ILLUSTRATOR
Leonard Everett Fisher
PUBLISHER
Holiday House
PUBLICATION DATE
1988
ILLUSTRATION MEDIUM
Acrylic

"The purpose here is simple enough—to see the images from a distance—to evoke a sense of eternally vast space and movement of the mysteries within, without artistic clutter."

BOOK TITLE
Prince Henry the Navigator
AUTHOR
Leonard Everett Fisher
ILLUSTRATOR
Leonard Everett Fisher
PUBLISHER
Macmillan Publishing Co.
PUBLICATION DATE
1990
ILLUSTRATION MEDIUM
Acrylic

"*I constantly strive to produce a work of art regardless of the subject or material at hand. Moreover, I render according to purpose and to effect a monumentality that is at once indelibly artistic and intellectually impressionable. In the case of 'Henry,' I was dealing with a singular, brooding, majestic historical person who imposed his will on an unsuspecting world, forever changing the world's perception of itself (i.e., the Ages of Exploration and Discovery). To have rendered this in high color or decoratively stylistic would have belied Henry's nature and eroded the focus of his intent. Thus the stark black, gray, and whiteness of the art.*"

BOOK TITLE
Pyramid of the Sun, Pyramid of the Moon
AUTHOR
Leonard Everett Fisher
ILLUSTRATOR
Leonard Everett Fisher
PUBLISHER
Macmillan Publishing Co.
PUBLICATION DATE
1988
ILLUSTRATION MEDIUM
Acrylic

"*My intent was to portray a moment in human affairs that was at once powerfully and mysteriously sacred—and to depict a wrenching, shuddering cultural change. In my view the communication of such events in black-and-white paint evokes the drama of such history and sends forth to the mind of the reader (or viewer) an indelible artistic image.*"

Paul Galdone
(1914–1986)

BOOK TITLE
What's in Fox's Sack?
AUTHOR
Retold by Paul Galdone
ILLUSTRATOR
Paul Galdone
PUBLISHER
Clarion Books
PUBLICATION DATE
1982

Author/illustrator Paul Galdone was born in Budapest, Hungary, and emigrated to the U.S. in 1928 where he studied art in the evenings at the Art Students League and the New York School of Industrial Design. He spent four years in the art department at Doubleday and Company where he had the opportunity to design his first book jacket. Following WWII he found himself in increasing demand as a freelance book illustrator. It was *Anatole,* the story of a French mouse, written by Eve Titus and published in 1956, that launched his success. Inspired by Arthur Rackham, Walter Crane and Dore, he particularly enjoyed adapting and making picture books of favorite old tales. In all, he illustrated nearly 300 books, many of which he wrote.

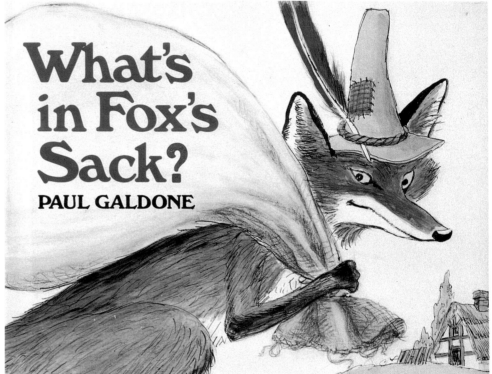

BOOK TITLE
Rumpelstiltskin
AUTHOR
Retold by Paul Galdone
ILLUSTRATOR
Paul Galdone
PUBLISHER
Clarion Books
PUBLICATION DATE
1985

Arthur Geisert

A graduate of Concordia College in Seward, Nebraska, Arthur Geisert earned his M.A. at the University of California at Davis in 1965 and then went on to study at the Choinard and Otis Art Institutes in Los Angeles and at the Chicago Art Institute. His work has been featured in solo shows in Washington, D.C., Boston and Philadelphia. In 1984 he wrote and illustrated his first children's book, *Pa's Balloon and other Pig Tales.* His award-winning *Pigs A to Z,* which he both wrote and illustrated, received a *New York Times* Best Illustrated Children's Book Award in 1986 and was published in Japanese in 1989.

BOOK TITLE
Oink
AUTHOR
Arthur Geisert
ILLUSTRATOR
Arthur Geisert
PUBLISHER
Houghton Mifflin
PUBLICATION DATE
1991
ILLUSTRATION MEDIUM
Etching, color overlay
PHOTOGRAPHER
Bill McConnell

BOOK TITLE
Pigs A to Z
AUTHOR
Arthur Geisert
ILLUSTRATOR
Arthur Geisert
PUBLISHER
Houghton Mifflin
PUBLICATION DATE
1986
ILLUSTRATION MEDIUM
Etching
PHOTOGRAPHER
Bill McConnell

"I try to combine a classical etching style (Piranesi, Rembrandt, Callot, etc.) with humor and narrative. The humor is funnier because of the seriousness, almost stodginess, of the etching technique."

Roy Gerrard

Born in Lancashire, England, in 1935, Roy Gerrard studied at Salford School of Art where he earned a National Diploma in Art and Design. He worked as an art teacher in secondary schools until he left teaching to paint and work on children's books. His illustrations were exhibited at the Bologna Book Fair in 1991 and his work has been shown in solo exhibitions in London, New Orleans, and Atlanta. Among Mr. Gerrard's awards are three from the Royal Academy of Arts, two *Parents' Choice* awards and several appearances on *The New York Times* Best Illustrated Children's Books list.

BOOK TITLE	PUBLISHER
Rosie and the Rustlers	**Victor Gollancz, London**
AUTHOR	**Farrar, Straus & Giroux**
Roy Gerrard	**New York**
ILLUSTRATOR	*PUBLICATION DATE*
Roy Gerrard	**1989**
	ILLUSTRATION MEDIUM
	Watercolor

"I'm sure the best reason for doing a book is to enjoy one's self and hope the enjoyment is communicated. I was raised on cowboy films and I enjoyed getting them out of my system. I made drawings of the local countryside and dramatized them to look like the Wild West, mainly by altering proportions. I would hope children would like the characters in the books as much as I do."

"The watercolor medium is inevitable."

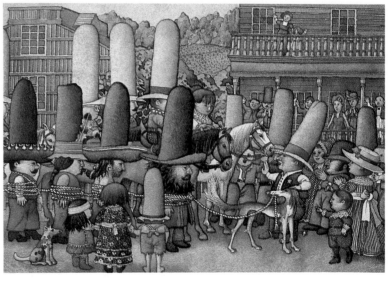

BOOK TITLE
Sir Cedric
AUTHOR
Roy Gerrard
ILLUSTRATOR
Roy Gerrard
PUBLISHER
**Victor Gollancz, London
Farrar, Straus & Giroux
New York**
PUBLICATION DATE
1984
ILLUSTRATION MEDIUM
Watercolor

"Sir Cedric owes his existence to my liking for medieval art, also to the visual absurdity of armor and accoutrements of the period. The book's landscapes were inspired by a 13th-century ruined castle near my home, set on a dramatic rock outcrop towering above small farmhouses, cottages and well-manicured rural land."

"The purpose of the book is to entertain and, hopefully, instruct. I use watercolor simply because I love it."

BOOK TITLE
Sir Francis Drake
AUTHOR
Roy Gerrard
ILLUSTRATOR
Roy Gerrard

PUBLISHER
**Victor Gollancz, London
Farrar, Straus & Giroux,
New York**
PUBLICATION DATE
1988
ILLUSTRATION MEDIUM
Watercolor

"An attempt to produce an entertainingly different version of a well-worn story, with a certain amount of affectionate mockery. The main problem was telescoping Drake's active and adventurous life into a short book. I hope the readers will feel the admiration I felt for Francis—he seemed astonishingly brave and also humane."

"Watercolor is simply my natural medium."

Diane Goode

Diane Goode, nee Capuozzo, was born in New York City and studied Fine Arts at Queens College and at Les Beaux Arts in Aix-en-Provence. She taught high school in New York City and illustration at U.C.L.A. In 1974 she began illustrating and has published over two dozen picture books. She has also translated stories from France and written two story books. Among her many awards are a Caldecott Honor for *When I Was Young in the Mountains* and numerous ALA Notable awards.

BOOK TITLE
When I Was Young in the Mountains
AUTHOR
Cynthia Rylant
ILLUSTRATOR
Diane Goode
PUBLISHER
Dutton Children's Books
PUBLICATION DATE
1982
ILLUSTRATION MEDIUM
Watercolor

"*This book was very difficult because it depicted a time and place unknown to most modern readers. It also spoke of a dignity and joy that can be found even in impoverishment. I wanted to make this understandable to young readers.*"

"*I used soft, muted colors to capture the atmosphere of Appalachia and the simplicity of this life. I felt that it was not necessary to live this life in order to understand the universal feeling of love...I hoped that by focusing in on intimate moments of life, one could share these feelings.*"

BOOK TITLE
Watch the Stars Come Out
AUTHOR
Riki Levinson
ILLUSTRATOR
Diane Goode
PUBLISHER
Dutton Children's Books
PUBLICATION DATE
1985
ILLUSTRATION MEDIUM
Watercolor, gouache and color pencil

"*In a story such as this one, you must be particularly careful not to over-romanticize or over sentimentalize. The story is told in retrospect and yet the reader must feel very present. I used a soft palette and texture in order to give the sense of an old photograph. By contrast the two children are very alive and it is through them that we experience the voyage. I wanted to contrast the harshness and seriousness of immigration with the way a child might experience it...as a great adventure.*"

BOOK TITLE
Where's Our Mama?
AUTHOR
Diane Goode
ILLUSTRATOR
Diane Goode
PUBLISHER
Dutton Children's Books
PUBLICATION DATE
1991
ILLUSTRATION MEDIUM
Watercolor and gouache

"*The problem here was logically and naturally to link one woman to the next. It was necessary to use a map of Paris to select a train station that was in walking distance to each site visited...The Gare d'Orsay was located off the Quay and the three could easily encounter all the women.*"

"*While the children obviously think their mother is the most wonderful woman in the world (a twist on, 'My father is stronger than your father'), I wanted to be sure not to elevate women at the expense of men and to avoid obvious stereotypes...for example the Diva is titanic but she is also glamorous and gorgeous.*"

"*The art for this story is much looser than my earlier books; I wanted to capture the action and excitement of Paris. I wanted most of all to capture the sense of unqualified love that children feel for their parents and the pure joy that they find when they are reunited.*"

BOOK TITLE
I Go with My Family to Grandma's
AUTHOR
Riki Levinson
ILLUSTRATOR
Diane Goode
PUBLISHER
Dutton Children's Books
PUBLICATION DATE
1986
ILLUSTRATION MEDIUM
Watercolor, gouache and color pencil

"*I hoped this book would bring to life a time gone by in our recent history. The text is wonderfully simple and I wanted to expand on it by giving a glimpse into the life of each family...where they lived, how they interacted, etc. So a simple text evolved into an extremely complex pictoral history. I kept track of each family through hair color and clothing in order to let the reader identify them on each page...I tried to give each family a personality.*"

"*I tried to keep the colors within sepia tones in order to evoke old photos.*"

Ann Grifalconi

A graduate of Cooper Union Art School and a resident of New York City, Ann Grifalconi has illustrated more than fifty children's books, seven of which she has authored. On a visit to Africa several years ago, she encountered a village where the women lived in round houses and the men in square ones. That real place and the story of its people became the basis of *The Village of Round and Square Houses,* a Caldecott Honor Book for 1987 and a *School Library Journal* Best Book of 1986. Her purpose in writing and illustrating the book was "to show that variations in human life do exist, do work, and that there are infinite creative solutions in the world."

"I wanted to create a sense of another 'real' place, to recreate the village and its people that I had actually visited in remote West Africa, especially because its unusual custom of housing—men in square houses, women and children in round ones—was a rare and successful experiment in human relations."

"I wanted to bring this to our own children to show that there are many ways to live. I wanted to show that myth and storytelling are very much alive in Africa, as well as in many other so-called third world countries, where people are still in touch with their beginnings and with each other."

"To bring all of this warmly and imaginatively to life, I used a 'rich' color palette, panoramas of land, houses, people, daily customs of sharing food, farming and other tasks."

"I hope the book evokes mystery, wonder, pleasure and identification."

BOOK TITLE
The Village of Round and Square Houses
AUTHOR
Ann Grifalconi
ILLUSTRATOR
Ann Grifalconi
PUBLISHER
Little, Brown and Company
PUBLICATION DATE
1906
ILLUSTRATION MEDIUM
Mixed media: chalk, colored pencil/wash

Helme Heine

Born in Berlin in 1941, Helme Heine has lived most of his life in Africa working as a stage designer, actor and director. He has run both a satirical magazine and a cabaret. In 1977 he moved to Munich. Helme Heine's books have been among *The New York Times* Best Illustrated Children's Books, and in 1984 he held the distinction of being named a runner-up for the international Hans Christian Andersen Award.

BOOK TITLE
The Most Wonderful Egg in the World
AUTHOR
Helme Heine
ILLUSTRATOR
Helme Heine
PUBLISHER
Margaret K. McElderry Books
PUBLICATION DATE
1983
ILLUSTRATION MEDIUM
Watercolor

"This book wants to show that beauty is something very individual — depending on personal taste, education, culture and preference."

"In contrast to our language of superlatives (the biggest, the richest, the prettiest, etc.), the illustrations are simple."

BOOK TITLE
Friends
AUTHOR
Helme Heine
ILLUSTRATOR
Helme Heine
PUBLISHER
Margaret K. McElderry Books
PUBLICATION DATE
1982
ILLUSTRATION MEDIUM
Watercolor

"*Besides showing the adventures of the three friends, the main aim is to find the secrets of friendship, in general. It shows the possibilities, the beauty, the philosophical aspects and the absolute need for friendship. But it also reminds us of its limitations and its problems.*"

"*The visual symbol of friendship in this book is the bicycle: none of the three friends can ride it on his own. It transforms three individuals into three friends who depend on one another and who trust each other.*"

But that night they dreamed about each other, the way true friends do.

Kevin Henkes

Kevin Henkes was born in Racine, Wisconsin, in 1960. His first book was accepted for publication when he was 19 years old. Since then he has written and illustrated 17 books for children, including both picture books and novels. He studied art at the University of Wisconsin, Madison. He currently lives in Madison with his wife.

Photo: Tom Beckley

BOOK TITLE
Julius, the Baby of the World
AUTHOR
Kevin Henkes
ILLUSTRATOR
Kevin Henkes
PUBLISHER
Greenwillow Books
PUBLICATION DATE
1990
ILLUSTRATION MEDIUM
Pen and ink/watercolor

BOOK TITLE
Chester's Way
AUTHOR
Kevin Henkes
ILLUSTRATOR
Kevin Henkes
PUBLISHER
Greenwillow Books
PUBLICATION DATE
1988
ILLUSTRATION MEDIUM
Pen and ink/watercolor

"Typically my drawings are pen-and-ink drawings combined with watercolor washes. I like the look of strong black lines, and I've liked working with watercolors for as long as I can remember."

BOOK TITLE
Jessica
AUTHOR
Kevin Henkes
ILLUSTRATOR
Kevin Henkes
PUBLISHER
Greenwillow Books
PUBLICATION DATE
1989
ILLUSTRATION MEDIUM
Pen and ink/watercolor

Ronald Himler

Ronald Himler is a native of Cleveland, Ohio. He studied painting at the Cleveland Institute of Art and Cranbrook Academy in Bloomfield Hills, Michigan, with academic credits from Hunter College and New York University. While holding various positions in the art field, he traveled extensively in Europe and Scandanavia, researching the major museums: the Louvre, the Uffizi Galleries and the Rijksmuseum in Amsterdam. He began his career as a children's book illustrator in 1970. Since that time he has authored and illustrated two books of his own, co-authored and illustrated a book with his wife, and illustrated over 50 books for children. Mr. Himler's books have been among the Best Book selections of the *School Library Journal,* The New York Public Library, and have been designated Notable Books by the American Library Association. *The Wall* was a 1991 *Horn Book* Fanfare Selection and also made the Master List of the Texas Bluebonnet Award.

"*T*he black-and-white format of the book was an economic decision of the publisher. Within that format, my task was to show the relationship between two people and the land on which they struggled to make a home. The pen-and-ink medium tends to give a hard-edged look, somewhat impersonal. But by mixing in pencil I tried to give the book an old-time look of early prints, but with a softness and warmth that allowed the reader to feel the story."

BOOK TITLE
Dakota Dugout
AUTHOR
Ann Turner
ILLUSTRATOR
Ronald Himler
PUBLISHER
Macmillan Publishing Co.
PUBLICATION DATE
1985
ILLUSTRATION MEDIUM
Pencil and pen and ink

"*One of the difficulties I encountered when illustrating the book was the subject itself. Since the book concerned the Vietnam Wall, each illustration would have to include this dark marble slab. The book itself would then have a dark, heavy look to it which I did not want.*"

"*To alleviate this visual problem, I chose to work in watercolors, lightening the wall with washes and reflections. This allowed me to focus on the relationships between people included in the story. I tried to do this in such a way as to evoke thoughtfulness without sentimentality.*"

BOOK TITLE
The Wall
AUTHOR
Eve Bunting
ILLUSTRATOR
Ronald Himler
PUBLISHER
Clarion Books
PUBLICATION DATE
1990
ILLUSTRATION MEDIUM
Watercolor and gouache

BOOK TITLE
Fly Away Home
AUTHOR
Eve Bunting
ILLUSTRATOR
Ronald Himler
PUBLISHER
Clarion Books
PUBLICATION DATE
1991
ILLUSTRATION MEDIUM
Watercolor and gouache

"*The real challenge of this book was to deal with a difficult, emotional theme, the plight of the homeless, with care and feeling. I wanted readers to have impressions that would help them form their own thoughts and feelings on the subject, rather than imposing my own views upon them.*"

"*To do this, I focused on three types of relationships, those between the main characters, the non-relationship between the homeless and background characters in the airport (travelers), and the effect of the impersonal surroundings of the airport itself.*"

"*Watercolor is a sensitive medium for treating a sensitive subject. The addition of gouache in certain areas of each illustration helped to give a hard edge to the reality of the story.*"

Pat Hutchins

Born in Yorkshire, England, Pat Hutchins was educated at Darlington College of Art, majoring in illustration at Leeds College of Art. The author/illustrator of 24 picture books and author of 5 novels for older readers, Ms. Hutchins won the Kate Greenaway Award for the best British children's book in 1974 for *The Wind Blew*. Her work has been widely exhibited in Britain and Japan.

BOOK TITLE
Rosie's Walk
AUTHOR
Pat Hutchins
ILLUSTRATOR
Pat Hutchins
PUBLISHER
Macmillan Publishing Co.
PUBLICATION DATE
1968
ILLUSTRATION MEDIUM
Pre-separated artwork

"*In* Rosie's Walk, *I tried to get the reader involved at the very beginning of the story. They know Rosie is being followed, Rosie does not.*"

"*I set up the pitfalls for the fox, so that the reader, by turning the page, actually makes the action happen. I tried to present the story so that the youngest child, who hadn't yet learned to decipher the squiggles that are words, could 'read' the book by the pictures.*"

BOOK TITLE
Changes, Changes
AUTHOR
Pat Hutchins
ILLUSTRATOR
Pat Hutchins
PUBLISHER
Macmillan Publishing Co.
PUBLICATION DATE
1971
ILLUSTRATION MEDIUM
Pre-separated artwork

"*I wanted to do a 'circular' book, where an object went through a series of transformations, and eventually ended up the same shape as it started from. I was watching my son playing with his building blocks, and decided that the use of blocks was the best way to present my idea.*"

"*As the story is in the pictures, I kept the book wordless. I used exactly the same blocks for all the different objects—otherwise it would have been cheating.*"

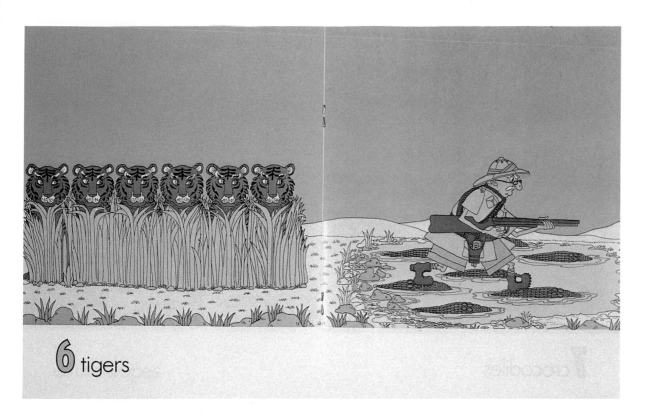

6 tigers

BOOK TITLE
1 Hunter
AUTHOR
Pat Hutchins
ILLUSTRATOR
Pat Hutchins
PUBLISHER
Greenwillow Books
PUBLICATION DATE
1982
ILLUSTRATION MEDIUM
Pre-separated artwork

"The problem with a counting book is that the items to be counted need to stand out as a 'pattern' on the page. I initially tried painting 1 Hunter in full color, but it didn't work—the animals blended in with the background too much, and it would have been difficult for a small child to pick out the characters to be counted. By using a black outline and flat color, I stylized the animals so they became 'units' that could be counted easily."

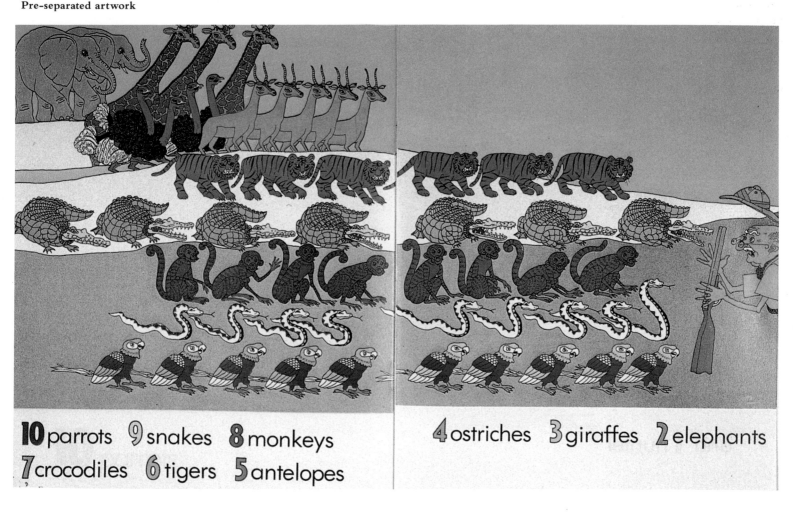

10 parrots   9 snakes   8 monkeys
7 crocodiles   6 tigers   5 antelopes

4 ostriches   3 giraffes   2 elephants

Warwick Hutton

BOOK TITLE
Jonah and the Great Fish
AUTHOR
Warwick Hutton
ILLUSTRATOR
Warwick Hutton
PUBLISHER
Margaret K. McElderry Books
PUBLICATION DATE
1984
ILLUSTRATION MEDIUM
Watercolor

Born in London of artist parents from New Zealand, Warwick Hutton lead a fairly nomadic existence, living in Suffolk, Wales, London and Essex, while his father worked as a mural painter and glass engraver. Warwick trained at the art school in Colchester, then as assistant in his father's London studio as he gradually built up his own freelance work. Since leaving art school, Mr. Hutton has worked in many branches of the art business, including portrait painting, TV graphics, photography, printmaking, glass engraving, painting and teaching. However, his original interest and training as an illustrator has gradually become a major focus of his work.

"I found to my surprise when I read the Bible carefully that although this story is commonly called 'Jonah and the Whale,' a whale is never mentioned. It is a great fish that swallows Jonah. When I looked further I realized that whales don't occur in the Mediterranean. A Zoologist told me that a whale's throat is too small to swallow a man in any case, so whales were thrown out. I bought a whiting from the fish merchant, propped it's mouth open with a matchstick and began to draw..."

BOOK TITLE
Beauty and the Beast
AUTHOR
Warwick Hutton
ILLUSTRATOR
Warwick Hutton
PUBLISHER
Margaret K. McElderry Books
PUBLICATION DATE
1985
ILLUSTRATION MEDIUM
Watercolor

"Beauty and the Beast is not a simple fairy story, it has many overtones of threat and loneliness. I have tried to use pictures with strong shadows to show drama and threat, and for loneliness there are many comparisons or tricks of scale. I think that a lot of the devices I use are instinctive, but I know this book is full of them, unusual perspective, contrasts of scale, effects of light, Moorish patterns to give a feeling of the Exotic."

BOOK TITLE
Theseus and the Minotaur
AUTHOR
Warwick Hutton
ILLUSTRATOR
Warwick Hutton
PUBLISHER
Margaret K. McElderry Books
PUBLICATION DATE
1989
ILLUSTRATION MEDIUM
Watercolor

"For this story I went to Crete to draw, all the landscapes are actual Cretan landscapes, details and costumes are researched in the Museum at Herakleion. Above all this is a story of Ancient Greece and the Mediterranean. I hope a feeling of sun, blue skies and seas, rocks and wild flowers provide a backdrop to a fast moving and exciting tale of monsters and escape, heroism and forgetfulness, which comes to us from many centuries in the past."

Trina Schart Hyman

Born in Philadelphia, Trina Schart Hyman attended the Philadelphia Museum School of Art (now Philadelphia College of Art), the Boston Museum School of Fine Arts and the Konstfackskolan (School for Applied Arts) in Stockholm, Sweden. Since her work premiered in 1961, she has illustrated approximately 130 books, four of which she has authored. From 1971–1978 she served as art director of *Cricket* magazine where she continued as staff artist until 1987, creating many of the "cricket and ladybug" characters. Ms. Hyman's many awards include the Caldecott Medal for *Saint George and the Dragon* in 1985, the *Boston Globe-Horn Book* Award, the Golden Kite Award, the Caldecott Honor Award for *Little Red Riding Hood* in 1985 and *Canterbury Tales* in 1989 and the Keene State College Children's Literature Award in 1991.

BOOK TITLE
Saint George and the Dragon
AUTHOR
Margaret Hodges
ILLUSTRATOR
Trina Schart Hyman
PUBLISHER
Little, Brown & Co.
PUBLICATION DATE
1984

ILLUSTRATION MEDIUM
India ink and acrylics on Windsor Newton Museum Board
PHOTOGRAPHER
Barbara Rogasky

"*I wanted to make the setting and atmosphere as authentic as I could (pre-Arthurian, pre-Norman Conquest England), so I did a tremendous amount of research into a period that is very sketchily documented. The red borders on each page are to symbolize the red cross—the flowers on the borders on the text pages are all indigenous to England and the British Isles. The dragon is very thoroughly described in the text, but otherwise is from my imagination. My goal was to try and evoke a time so long ago that magic and reality were equally plausible.*"

BOOK TITLE
The Kitchen Knight
AUTHOR
Margaret Hodges
ILLUSTRATOR
Trina Schart Hyman
PUBLISHER
Holiday House
PUBLICATION DATE
1990
ILLUSTRATION MEDIUM
**India ink and acrylics on
Bainbridge Board**
PHOTOGRAPHER
Barbara Rogasky

"*This was a difficult book to design, because there's so much action going on in the story—it was hard to make decisions about which incidents should get picture preference. I finally found the solution in a book of illuminated manuscripts from the fourteenth century—the device of a picture within a picture; a small detail of the larger 'action' overlaid on the main illustration. Because this is one of the Arthurian tales, the general feeling is similar to* Saint George and the Dragon, *but the atmosphere is much more robust and swashbuckling—more human interest, less fantasy.*"

BOOK TITLE
Little Red Riding Hood
AUTHOR
Retold by Trina Schart Hyman
ILLUSTRATOR
Trina Schart Hyman
PUBLISHER
Holiday House
PUBLICATION DATE
1983

ILLUSTRATION MEDIUM
**India ink and acrylics on
Bainbridge Board**
PHOTOGRAPHER
Barbara Rogasky

"Little Red Riding Hood *was my favorite story when I was a very little girl, and it was the first book I learned to read. I identified so strongly with Little Red that my mother finally gave in and made me a Little Red cape with a hood, and I spent my days being Little Red Riding Hood."*

"I illustrated the story with this in mind—Little Red is me, as I looked when I was four or five years old, and her mom and grandmother are my own, as they looked then. I set the story in my own New Hampshire village and forests, and the patterns in the borders are all from dresses I wore as a little girl. The cats are all cats I've had as pets, and the huntsman is my dear old neighbor Hugh O'Donnell. It's a personal statement—a kind of love letter to my own childhood and to day-dreamy, shy little kids everywhere."

Erick Ingraham

Born in Philadelphia, Erick Ingraham was influenced by his artistic mother, an elementary school teacher, and his father, a veterinarian, who provided him with the useful combination of exposure to culture and the desire to know how things work. He received his B.A. in fine arts/painting from Pennsylvania's Kutztown State College in 1972. In 1974 he began illustrating a wide spectrum of subjects in books, and today his art can be found in seven distinguished children's books. Among Mr. Ingraham's many awards are the American Book Award for *Porcupine Stew,* and a *Boston Globe-Horn Book* Honor Award for *Cross-Country Cat.*

BOOK TITLE
Hot-Air Henry
AUTHOR
Mary Calhoun
ILLUSTRATOR
Erick Ingraham
PUBLISHER
Morrow Junior Books
PUBLICATION DATE
1981
ILLUSTRATION MEDIUM
Pencil, ink, films on mylar

"Through 'on-location' photography research and a balloon flight, I was able to be more convincing with my viewer-angles and dramatic action. The 'Henry' books best display my life-long love of detailed pencil drawing through the pre-separation process; in this book, I also used flat-grey adhesive film, India ink and graphite dust on four layers of mylar sheets."

BOOK TITLE
High-Wire Henry
AUTHOR
Mary Calhoun
ILLUSTRATOR
Erick Ingraham
PUBLISHER
Morrow Junior Books
PUBLICATION DATE
1991
ILLUSTRATION MEDIUM
Watercolor and pencil

"*In* High-Wire Henry, *I was trying to weave together the look of the pre-separated art for* Cross-Country Cat *and* Hot-Air Henry *with the experience in watercolor I've gained in the years since. The artwork I produced for full-color reproduction was just as labor-intensive as the first books. From the 'scribbles' to the details, it was a long journey of refinement, but I loved every step of the way!*"

BOOK TITLE
Little Daylight
AUTHOR
George MacDonald
ILLUSTRATOR
Erick Ingraham
PUBLISHER
Morrow Junior Books
PUBLICATION DATE
1988
ILLUSTRATION MEDIUM
Acrylic

"I tried to create a mysteriously realistic setting by concentrating on lighting effects, model, costuming and the elements of nature. I painted this book over a long span of time using acrylic in a tempura style and used airbrush only when an effect was needed. I chose this tale mainly because it provided my favorite ingredient, contrast."

BOOK TITLE
Porcupine Stew
AUTHOR
Beverly Major
ILLUSTRATOR
Erick Ingraham
PUBLISHER
Morrow Junior Books
PUBLICATION DATE
1982
ILLUSTRATION MEDIUM
Acrylic on paper

"*H*aving the luxury of full-color and thrilled with expanding my skills into the acrylic medium, I went overboard with meticulous detail. I painted this book in airbrush and relied on fine brush work to refine it. The dense color and night scenes were a refreshing contrast to my bright, soft-colored books.*"*

Susan Jeffers

BOOK TITLE
Brother Eagle, Sister Sky: A Message from Chief Seattle
AUTHOR
Inspired by Chief Seattle
ILLUSTRATOR
Susan Jeffers

PUBLISHER
Dial Books for Young Readers
PUBLICATION DATE
1991
ILLUSTRATION MEDIUM
Pen and ink

The bear, the deer, the great eagle, these are our brothers.

Susan Jeffers attended Pratt Institute in Brooklyn and then worked in three publishing houses where she gained invaluable experience in how books are made. Working on other artists' books spurred her interest in children's literature and in creating books herself. She started her own design studio with author/illustrator Rosemary Wells to earn money while working on her first book, *The Buried Moon*. Her second book, *The Three Jovial Huntsmen*, was a Caldecott Honor Book, and her more recent books have been cited by virtually every children's award as outstanding books of the year.

"*This book includes images of great beauty and great destruction—a tremendous challenge to put in a children's book. It was first done with a great amount of research including trips to museums and locations in the Northwest, Southwest, and the East Coast. Original documents and paintings, artifacts, clothing and first-person accounts from the eras represented were used as reference.*"

"*The art was sketched in pencil first, a gouache transparently applied, and then a fine pen line with black or colored ink put down on top. My characters were drawn from Sioux friends who were gracious enough to pose.*"

The rocky crests, the meadows, the ponies—all belong to the same family.

85

BOOK TITLE
Three Jovial Huntsmen
AUTHOR
Mother Goose Rhyme
ILLUSTRATOR
Susan Jeffers
PUBLISHER
Bradbury Press
PUBLICATION DATE
1975
ILLUSTRATION MEDIUM
**Pen and ink, oil on
acetate overlays**

"*I was intrigued by the mysterious verse about things seen and unseen and how they were interpreted. It was so mysterious, though, that my first attempt ended in failure at the printing press. I decided then that I would never attempt another children's book. After a year of teaching at a school for disturbed children I was ready for another try. The second version benefited greatly from the long rest. My characters had become much more lighthearted and the colors full of atmosphere. I changed from opaque separations to thin pen and ink with transparent overlays done in oil.*"

All the day they hunted,
And nothing could they find,

Ann Jonas

Ann Jonas graduated from Cooper Union in 1959 and worked as a graphic designer, first on staff in design offices and then with her husband, Donald Crews. She began writing and illustrating children's books in 1981. *Round Trip, The Trek* and *Aardvarks, Disembark!* were all ALA Notable Books; *Round Trip* was also a *New York Times* Best Illustrated Children's Book and in the AIGA Book Show. Both *The Trek* and *Aardvarks, Disembark!* were *Boston Globe-Horn Book* Honor Books. Ann Jonas has spoken at many workshops and conventions and at schools and libraries around the country. Her work has been exhibited at the Henry Feiwel Gallery in New York and is in the Mazza Collection at Findlay College. In 1991 her work was exhibited at the Grand Rapids Art Museum and in 1990 it was included in a traveling exhibition in Japan titled "Picture Books Edited by Susan Hirschman."

BOOK TITLE
Aardvarks, Disembark!
AUTHOR
Ann Jonas
ILLUSTRATOR
Ann Jonas
PUBLISHER
Greenwillow Books
PUBLICATION DATE
1990
ILLUSTRATION MEDIUM
Line and watercolor

"*W*anting to do an animal alphabet book, using as many obscure animals as possible, I chose Noah's Ark as the vehicle. I started the story at the end of the flood so that I could focus on the animals leaving the ark, which Noah has them do in alphabetical order. Noah follows and overtakes them, which meant a reverse order for the alphabet, starting with the Zs. To enhance the feeling of descending the mountain, I turned the book to have it open from the bottom, so that animals appear to go down and down the mountain, increasing in size from page to page. The book was done in watercolor, with a holding line to enable me to show detail within the flat color. Since many of the animals are endangered, it also became an opportunity to heighten children's awareness of the diversity of animal life that we must protect."

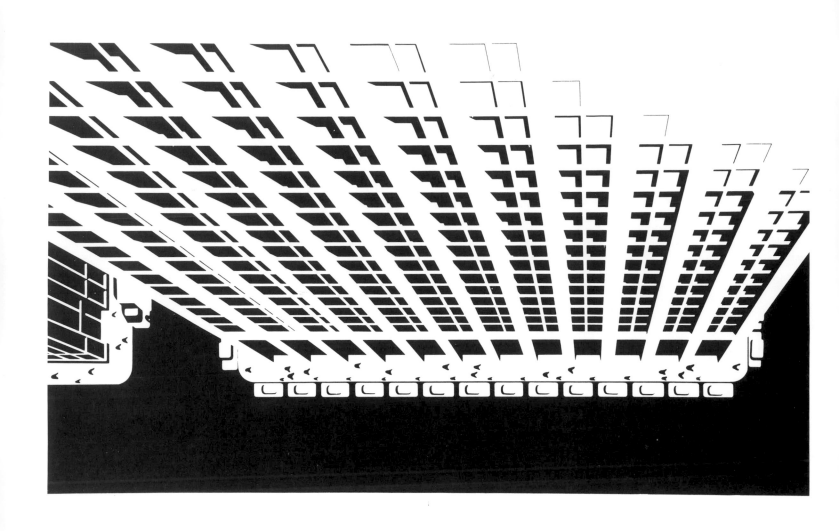

BOOK TITLE
The Trek
AUTHOR
Ann Jonas
ILLUSTRATOR
Ann Jonas
PUBLISHER
Greenwillow Books
PUBLICATION DATE
1985
ILLUSTRATION MEDIUM
Watercolor

BOOK TITLE	PUBLISHER
Round Trip	**Greenwillow Books**
AUTHOR	*PUBLICATION DATE*
Ann Jonas	**1983**
ILLUSTRATOR	*ILLUSTRATION MEDIUM*
Ann Jonas	**Black ink and gouache**

"Round Trip *was designed to be read through to the end, turned over and read back to the beginning. This meant creating illustrations that had two separate, but linked and intermeshed images. It also created many problems in finding perspectives that would work in each direction. Doing the book in black and white enabled me to emphasize the figure/ground aspect and abstract it further. Since it was difficult to find images that fit together, I planned all the illustrations first and then arranged them into a logical story sequence. Children seem to be stimulated to create their own figure/ground drawings after looking at the book.*"

"In The Trek, *I wanted to create a book of hidden animals, hiding them in familiar objects in such a way that a child would have to use his imagination to find them. I set the story as a child's walk to school alone, to suggest a time when his imagination might be in full play, and to give myself varied environments in which to hide the animals. I worked in watercolors, layering the color to control the degree of difficulty in finding the animals. Children seem to find the animals a little more easily than I intended; I guess their imaginations are unencumbered by preconceptions.*"

William Joyce

William Joyce, self-portrait

Award-winning illustrator and author William Joyce has completed more than a dozen outstanding children's books. His well-known *A Day With Wilbur Robinson* appeared on the cover of *Publishers Weekly* and was cited as one of the 50 Best Books in the World in *Interview* magazine, 1990. *Dinosaur Bob and His Adventures with the Family Lazardo* made the year end best list in *Time, Newsweek, Booklist* and *Publishers Weekly* magazines and was also a main selection on the PBS TV Series, "Reading Rainbow." Educated at Southern Methodist University in Texas, Mr. Joyce now resides in Shreveport, LA, where he recently initiated and coordinated The First Annual Red River International Film Festival.

BOOK TITLE
Dinosaur Bob and His Adventures with the Family Lazardo
AUTHOR
William Joyce
ILLUSTRATOR
William Joyce
PUBLISHER
HarperCollins
PUBLICATION DATE
1988
ILLUSTRATION MEDIUM
Acrylic

"*I never got over the fact that they killed King Kong or Old Yeller. Dinosaur Bob is my revenge on those heart-breakers of my childhood.*"

"*It seemed more plausible for the story of a dinosaur adopted by an American family to take place in some era other than the present, so in keeping with Kong and to give the book a very American tone, I set it in the Depression of the 1930s. For inspiration I studied Grant Wood and Edward Hopper. The delicate cross-hatching of acrylic especially favors Mr. Wood's work.*"

BOOK TITLE
A Day with Wilbur Robinson
AUTHOR
William Joyce
ILLUSTRATOR
William Joyce
PUBLISHER
HarperCollins
PUBLICATION DATE
1990
ILLUSTRATION MEDIUM
Acrylic

"*I grew up in a very eccentric home, though at the time I thought everybody's family was like ours. It wasn't until I began spending the night at friends' houses that I realized how distinct and singularly odd my own upbringing was. This was the nucleus of* Wilbur Robinson. *I wanted the illustrations to evoke the airy look of old science fiction movies and family photographs (the two were remarkably similar at my house), so I used thin washes of acrylic on Arches watercolor paper to get that feeling.*"

Ezra Jack Keats
(1916–1983)

The son of Polish immigrants, Ezra Jack Keats was born in Brooklyn during the Depression. As a child he spent hours at the Arlington Branch of the Brooklyn Public Library. His long and productive career yielded more than 80 books, 23 of which he both authored and illustrated. *The Snowy Day,* which won the Caldecott Medal in 1963, is considered a landmark book for its depictions of Black children at play in the inner city. The book also broke ground with its use of collage, a technique previously untried by Keats. *Goggles!* was a Caldecott Honor Book in 1970, and *Apt. 3* won the Gold Venus Medallion at the Virgin Islands International Film Festival in 1977. Keats' books have been published in 16 languages. In addition to his prolific output as an author/illustrator of children's books, Keats painted five Christmas cards for UNICEF and served as a consultant at conferences which helped formulate Sesame Street.

BOOK TITLE
Goggles!
AUTHOR
Ezra Jack Keats
ILLUSTRATOR
Ezra Jack Keats
PUBLISHER
Macmillan Publishing Co.
PUBLICATION DATE
1969
ILLUSTRATION MEDIUM
Multi-collage, paint and colored pencil on board

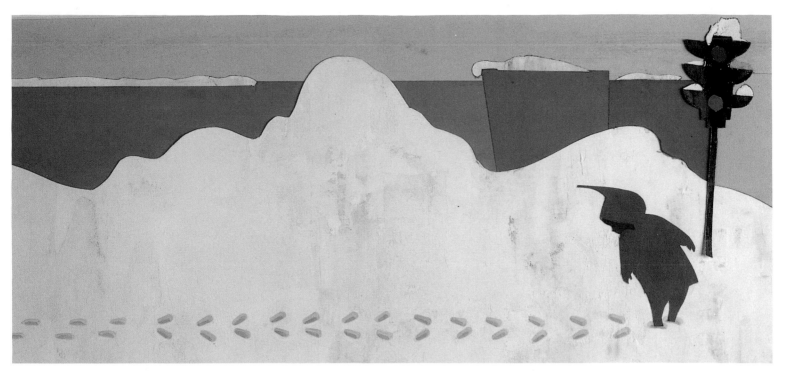

BOOK TITLE
The Snowy Day
AUTHOR
Ezra Jack Keats
ILLUSTRATOR
Ezra Jack Keats
PUBLISHER
Viking Press
PUBLICATION DATE
1962
ILLUSTRATION MEDIUM
Collage on board

"I decided to make Peter a Black child. I had been illustrating books by other people showing the goodness of white children, and in my own book I wanted to show and share the beauty and goodness of the Black child. I wanted the world to know that all children experience wonderful things in life. I wanted to convey the joy of being a little boy alive on a certain kind of day—of being for that moment. The air is cold, you touch the snow, aware of the things to which all children are so open."

"The combination of the purpose of the book and the subject matter of the book was so strong that my style changed completely. It turned out to be the beginning of a whole new style to me because I was so deeply involved."

BOOK TITLE
Apt. 3
AUTHOR
Ezra Jack Keats
ILLUSTRATOR
Ezra Jack Keats
PUBLISHER
Macmillan Publishing Co.
PUBLICATION DATE
1971
ILLUSTRATION MEDIUM
Paint on board with paper collage

Bert Kitchen

BOOK TITLE
Gorilla/Chinchilla
AUTHOR
Bert Kitchen
ILLUSTRATOR
Bert Kitchen
PUBLISHER
**Dial Books for Young Readers
New York
Jonathan Cape, London**
PUBLICATION DATE
1990
ILLUSTRATION MEDIUM
Watercolor and gouache

Born in Liverpool, Bert Kitchen attended Rochdale School of Art, Lancashire, and earned a Design Diploma from London Central School of Arts and Crafts. A painter for 30 years, it wasn't until he met Patrick Hardy in 1984 that he began writing and illustrating children's books. He has illustrated seven books and in 1991 was awarded the Gold Medal for Illustration from the Society of Illustrators, Museum of American Illustration. Mr. Kitchen is Visiting Lecturer for Drawing and Design at City of London Polytechnic and previously taught at London Central School of Arts and Crafts. His paintings have been widely exhibited in London, Japan and Germany and are in numerous private collections worldwide.

"I chose animals that would not only rhyme, but would also create unusual or surreal situations. Watercolor and gouache allowed me to achieve the credibility."

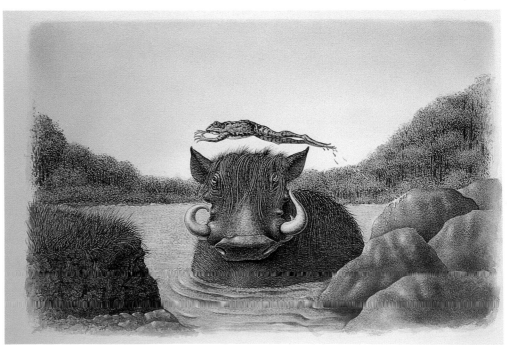

BOOK TITLE
Animal Numbers
AUTHOR
Bert Kitchen
ILLUSTRATOR
Bert Kitchen
PUBLISHER
Dial Books for Young Readers
New York
Lutterworth, Cambridge
PUBLICATION DATE
1987
ILLUSTRATION MEDIUM
Watercolor, gouache

"*It was an integral part of the design to relate the illustration to the numeral. The theme was based on the idea of the number of young ones animals have, and how they tend to behave toward the parent.*"

"*My initial idea was to relate each creature to its relative letter, by depicting the animal in its characteristic pose, using the letter as a sort of prop. Watercolors and gouache allowed me to achieve the 'presence.'*"

BOOK TITLE
Animal Alphabet
AUTHOR
Bert Kitchen
ILLUSTRATOR
Bert Kitchen
PUBLISHER
Dial Books for Young Readers
New York
Patrick Hardy Books, London
PUBLICATION DATE
1984
ILLUSTRATION MEDIUM
Watercolor and gouache

Leo Lionni

Born in 1910, Leo Lionni spent the first twelve years of his life in Amsterdam where he spent a great deal of time in art museums and formed an early resolve to become an artist. He attended the University of Zurich, emigrated to the U.S. in 1939 and worked as an art director for N.W. Ayer & Sons and *Fortune,* among others. He also headed the graphics design department for the Parsons School of Design and served as president of the American Institute of Graphic Arts. In 1958 he created his first children's book, *Little Blue and Little Yellow,* and from that time on he devoted his talent to writing and illustrating children's books. Among his many awards are the Lewis Carroll Shelf Award, the German Children's Book Prize, and the Golden Apple Award. His well-known *Inch by Inch, Swimmy,* and *Frederick* were all Caldecott Honor Books.

"*A*s someone who has chosen to be responsible for the totality of his picture books — the integration of words and images — I do not think of myself as an illustrator. Even the word illustration seems misleading. Although illustrations help to give form and color to verbal abstractions, the pictures should not merely illustrate but create a spatial environment for the story's action. They are in fact more like the scenery in the theatre, the stage sets in which the actors move and act."

"The little drama that became **Frederick** started one day in Italy as I was walking to my studio, a reconverted barn near our house. I found myself face to face (foot to face, actually) with a very frightened little fieldmouse. When it saw me it froze to its tiny feet, then jumped up and darted into the geraniums that flanked the flagstone path. Later, my eyes wandered along the shelves of my studio which were filled not only with books but with hundreds of objects I had collected on my travels around the world, and dozens of large round pebbles, as well. 'How much nonsense,' I thought, and I found myself saying, 'Once upon a time there was a little fieldmouse. All the other mice gathered nuts and berries for the winter ahead while he collected pebbles. "Why do you collect pebbles?" they asked annoyed. "You never know. They may come in handy someday," he answered mysteriously.'"

"In the case of **Frederick,** as in each of my books, I try to create a mood that is specific for the fictional character of the story. The prevalent cold gray color emphasizes by contrast the warmth of Frederick's words."

BOOK TITLE
Frederick
AUTHOR
Leo Lionni
ILLUSTRATOR
Leo Lionni
PUBLISHER
Pantheon Books
PUBLICATION DATE
1967
ILLUSTRATION MEDIUM
Colored paper

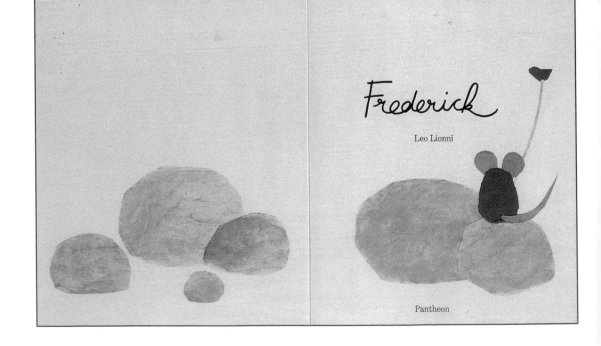

BOOK TITLE
Little Blue and Little Yellow
AUTHOR
Leo Lionni
ILLUSTRATOR
Leo Lionni
PUBLISHER
Astor-Honor, Inc.
PUBLICATION DATE
1959
ILLUSTRATION MEDIUM
Colored paper

there was little yellow!

Happily they hugged each other

"*With* Little Blue and Little Yellow *I did not set out to make a book but to entertain two restless grandchildren as we took a commuter train from New York to Connecticut. From* Life *magazine I tore a few small pieces of colored paper and improvised a story—the adventures of two colors. The children were glued to their seats and after a happy ending I had to start all over again. That evening, I made a rough dummy. My first book was born.*"

"*Little Blue is often described as an abstract book for children. It is not an abstract book. But neither is it 'realistic.' The characters don't look like people. They are blobs of color. But humanized. Not by adding arms and legs but by giving them shapes which derive from the stylization of our feelings. They are formal stereotypes. The children are little. The mother is round and shorter than the father, who is tall and thin. Children know who is who.*"

"*The mountain and the tunnel are analogs of real mountains and real tunnels. Although highly stylized, they are recognizable images.*"

"*In the houses and the school, form and color represent the feelings they evoke in us. We see and recognize them too. And so, miraculously, Little Blue and Little Yellow, nothing but blobs of color, are perceived from the very beginning as the protagonists of the story.*"

"*In this, as in all my books, I want the combination of words and image to provoke leaps of the imagination and stimulate children to fantasize on their own.*"

A happy school of little fish lived in a corner of the sea somewhere. They were all red. Only one of them was as black as a mussel shell. He swam faster than his brothers and sisters. His name was Swimmy.

BOOK TITLE
Swimmy
AUTHOR
Leo Lionni
ILLUSTRATOR
Leo Lionni
PUBLISHER
Pantheon Books
PUBLICATION DATE
1968
ILLUSTRATION MEDIUM
Watercolor

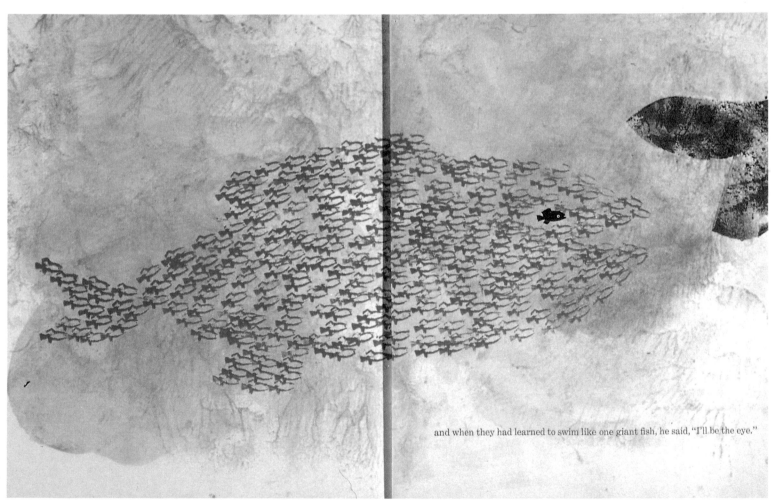

and when they had learned to swim like one giant fish, he said, "I'll be the eye."

"*For* Swimmy—*my fable about a social-political idealist who discovers the meaning of beauty as a life force—I wanted to find a medium to suggest the wet watery world of the deepsea. So I made watercolor monoprints, first painting on glass and then transferring the image directly to paper. The resulting images, vaguely allusive, well represent things seen in the shimmering light of the underwater worlds.*"

"Don't eat me. I am an inchworm. I am useful.
I measure things."
"Is that so!" said the robin. "Then measure my tail!"

BOOK TITLE
Inch by Inch
AUTHOR
Leo Lionni
ILLUSTRATOR
Leo Lionni

PUBLISHER
Astor-Honor, Inc.
PUBLICATION DATE
1960
ILLUSTRATION MEDIUM
Collage and crayon

"*When I set about doing a second book it became clear that it would have to be completely different in theme, style and technique from* Little Blue and Little Yellow. *After much creative turmoil I finally produced* Inch by Inch, *the story of an inch worm who measures birds and a hungry nightingale. It is a short, simple animal fable illustrated with large colorful collages. For these clearly representational collages I used many different papers on which I had first painted, printed and drawn. It was only several years (and books) later that I realized that* Inch by Inch *was the real forerunner of my fables, in which small animals can be the heroes and heroines of big events.*"

Anita Lobel

Anita Lobel was born in Cracow, Poland, and spent part of her childhood in a concentration camp. After the war, she came to the U.S. with her parents and won a scholarship to Pratt Institute. She became a textile designer, working at home while she and Arnold Lobel raised two small children. After completing her first picture book she came to the conclusion that weaving a story and pictures was more interesting than designing fabrics. She has written and illustrated dozens of books and has especially enjoyed illustrating stories written by Arnold Lobel. Her award-winning books include *On Market Street,* a 1982 Caldecott Honor Book, and *The Rose in My Garden,* a 1984 *Boston Globe-Horn Book* Honor Book.

BOOK TITLE
On Market Street
AUTHOR
Arnold Lóbel
ILLUSTRATOR
Anita Lobel
PUBLISHER
Greenwillow Books
PUBLICATION DATE
1981
ILLUSTRATION MEDIUM
Black penline and full color separation in watercolor

ice cream,

"The illustrations for this alphabet book are influenced by seventeenth-century engravings of tradespeople extravagantly costumed in the products and implements of their occupations."

BOOK TITLE
Alison's Zinnia
AUTHOR
Anita Lobel
ILLUSTRATOR
Anita Lobel
PUBLISHER
Greenwillow Books
PUBLICATION DATE
1990
ILLUSTRATION MEDIUM
Watercolor and gouache

Crystal cut a Chrysanthemum for Dawn.

C

"I love to draw and paint flowers. I worked on these 26 paintings for more than a year. In selecting the flowers, I picked first those I really wanted to paint, but I had to bow to the needs of the alphabet. Some flowers behaved like divas, while others took direction very well. The chorus of little girls, without exception, behaved splendidly."

Irene inked an Iris for Jane.

I

BOOK TITLE
Princess Furball
AUTHOR
Charlotte Huck
ILLUSTRATOR
Anita Lobel
PUBLISHER
Greenwillow Books
PUBLICATION DATE
1989
ILLUSTRATION MEDIUM
Gouache

"*When I read this manuscript I saw a series of imprisoning enclosures that the Princess passes through on her journey from darkness to light. Next, I came upon the idea of using portraits to personify characters that would otherwise remain invisible. This idea was especially useful when the ogre came into the story.*"

"*I suggested the passage of time by the waxing moon peeping in through various windows. The moon is full when the Princess sheds her fur at last and the King declares his love for her.*"

"*The last picture had to be a portrait to show a summary of past and future. The colors worn by each member of the royal family echo those worn on other occasions throughout the story.*"

Arnold Lobel
(1933–1987)

Photo: Van Williams

BOOK TITLE
Fables
AUTHOR
Arnold Lobel
ILLUSTRATOR
Arnold Lobel
PUBLISHER
HarperCollins
PUBLICATION DATE
1980
ILLUSTRATION MEDIUM
Gouache

Arnold Lobel was born in Los Angeles, California, grew up in Schenectady, New York, and attended Pratt Institute in Brooklyn. During his distinguished career, he wrote and/or illustrated over 70 books for children. Among his outstanding achievements are the Caldecott Medal for *Fables* in 1981, and several Caldecott Honor Books, including *Frog and Toad Are Friends* and *Hildilid's Night*. In 1977 Mr. Lobel and his wife, Anita, collaborated on their first book, *How the Rooster Saved the Day,* chosen by *School Library Journal* as one of the Best Books of the Year. In 1973, the Bank Street College of Education presented the first Irma Simonton Black Award to Mr. Lobel for *Mouse Tales* (an *I Can Read* Book).

BOOK TITLE
The Book of Pigericks
AUTHOR
Arnold Lobel
ILLUSTRATOR
Arnold Lobel
PUBLISHER
HarperCollins
PUBLICATION DATE
1983
ILLUSTRATION MEDIUM
Watercolor and pencil with occasional thin penline

BOOK TITLE
**The Headless Horseman Rides
Tonight**
AUTHOR
Jack Prelutsky
ILLUSTRATOR
Arnold Lobel
PUBLISHER
Greenwillow Books
PUBLICATION DATE
1980
ILLUSTRATION MEDIUM
Pen and ink

Suse MacDonald
Bill Oakes

Suse MacDonald grew up in Glencoe, Illinois, and earned a B.A. from the State University of Iowa. Her early art training included five years as a textbook illustrator and ten years as a draftsperson and designer. She studied at the New England School of Art and Design, the Art Institute and the Radcliffe Seminar Program. In 1987 her first children's book, *Alphabatics,* won a Caldecott Honor and the Golden Kite Award from the Society of Children's Book Writers. In collaboration with Bill Oakes, she has written and illustrated *Numblers, Puzzlers,* and *Once Upon Another.* In addition to writing and illustrating, Suse MacDonald is a frequent lecturer at schools, libraries and professional conferences.

An artist, author and teacher, Bill Oakes uses art and visual thinking as creative problem-solving tools. He holds a master's degree in critical and creative thinking from the University of Massachusetts and is currently developing an exhibit of non-objective paintings that demonstrate painting from the intuitive side of thought. In addition to teaching courses in painting, Mr. Oakes teaches a course in the creation of children's books and a course called "Connectivity, the Handle for Nurturing Creative Leaps" for teachers who want to be facilitators for discovery in their classrooms. He has also created a design for a children's TV series that will involve the audience in the creative process.

"*Once Upon Another is a novel and spirited retelling of two fables. Both* The Lion and The Mouse *and* The Tortoise and the Hare *are illustrated with the same abstract pictures. When the reader arrives at the end of one tale the book is turned upside down to begin the next. The reader is challenged to make a meaningful connection between the story and the art which is an abstract representation of the story.*"

"*Our biggest challenge was to find two stories that would fit together. They had to have the same number of characters and be approximately the same length. Each illustration was designed so that it would be meaningful for the appropriate text of each tale.*"

"*Paper collage was the medium chosen because it allowed us to work simultaneously on creating each piece of artwork. The paper pieces for each illustration could also be cut out and arranged for viewing but not glued down until the entire book was ready.*"

"*Our aim in this book is to point children's art in a new direction. By using abstract shapes to illustrate a story, we give readers the opportunity to use their own imaginations to make the stories real.*"

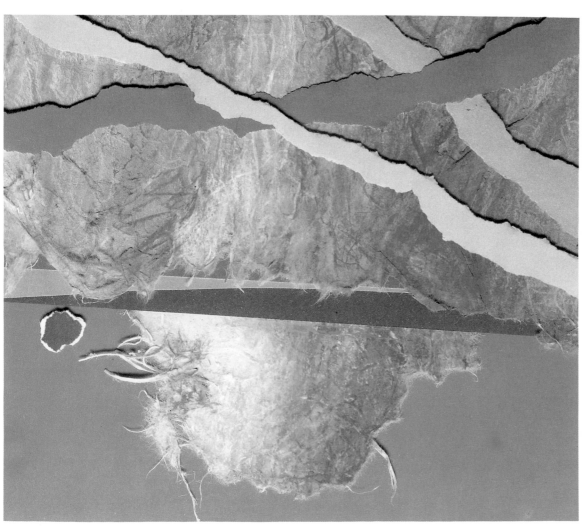

BOOK TITLE
Once Upon Another
AUTHOR
Suse MacDonald and Bill Oakes
ILLUSTRATOR
Suse MacDonald and Bill Oakes
PUBLISHER
Dial Books for Young Readers
PUBLICATION DATE
1990
ILLUSTRATION MEDIUM
Paper collage

BOOK TITLE
Numblers
AUTHOR
Suse MacDonald and Bill Oakes
ILLUSTRATOR
Suse MacDonald and Bill Oakes
PUBLISHER
Dial Books for Young Readers
PUBLICATION DATE
1988
ILLUSTRATION MEDIUM
Paper collage

"Numblers *is a collaborative effort. Working from the premise that children learn most quickly and effectively through a process of discovery, we created a format for discovery by the reader.*"

"*Each double page spread shows the transformation of a numeral between one and ten into an image which is suggested by the shape of the numeral and which is familiar to the reader. This transformation encourages a child to make a connection between a number, which is an abstract concept, and something concrete which he or she knows. A 4 becomes a fast-moving sailboat made up of four 4s. Nine 9s get together to become a squirrel. In a like manner the other numbers twist and reform into colorful new images.*"

"*Brilliantly colored paper collages animate each sequence of changes. We used papers that were hand-colored with textures that give the feeling of each animal or object. The numerals which make up the image were cut from this paper and glued to a colorful background. Young readers delight in the sharp graphics and imaginative shapes as they count the number of parts in each picture.*"

James Marshall

Born in Texas in 1942, James Marshall excelled as a musician, playing both the violin and the viola until a hand injury in 1961 eliminated the possibility of a musical career. He earned a degree in history and began writing and illustrating full time after illustrating his first book, *Plink, Plink, Plink*. His first solo effort resulted in the well-known *George and Martha* series, the story of two loveable hippos and their friendship. Collaborating with Harry Allard he created the Stupid Family and the character of Viola Swamp who appears in *Miss Nelson is Missing!* and subsequent Miss Nelson books. Recognized for character illustration and development, James Marshall makes preliminary doodles as he works and then tries to put his character into a situation that he would be least likely to be in, thus avoiding a resolution that is conventional.

BOOK TITLE
George and Martha Encore
AUTHOR
James Marshall
ILLUSTRATOR
James Marshall
PUBLISHER
Houghton Mifflin Company
PUBLICATION DATE
1973

BOOK TITLE
Miss Nelson is Missing!
AUTHOR
Harry Allard
ILLUSTRATOR
James Marshall
PUBLISHER
Houghton Mifflin Company
PUBLICATION DATE
1977

BOOK TITLE
Red Riding Hood
AUTHOR
Retold by James Marshall
ILLUSTRATOR
James Marshall
PUBLISHER
Dial Books for Young Readers
PUBLICATION DATE
1987

Petra Mathers

Photo: Michael Mathers

"In 1983 I illustrated my first children's book. In black and white. Now I work in living color. I like to illustrate my own books best, since I already met the cast of characters when I wrote it."

Petra Mathers received the Ezra Jack Keats Memorial Award for *Maria Theresa* in 1986. Three of her books have won *The New York Times* Best Illustrated Children's Book Award: *Molly's New Washing Machine* (1986); *Theodor and Mr. Balbini* (1988); and *I'm Flying* (1990).

BOOK TITLE
Sophie and Lou
AUTHOR
Petra Mathers
ILLUSTRATOR
Petra Mathers
PUBLISHER
HarperCollins
PUBLICATION DATE
1991

114

ILLUSTRATION MEDIUM
Watercolor
PHOTOGRAPHER
Michael Mathers

"*Sophie is shy but she is also very brave. She has enormous dignity and could have done very well on her own. But she was curious and knew there was more to life than a dust-free house. By painting the dancing steps on her floor she abandoned all that. Sophie is not cute. I wanted her removed—you may observe her but don't touch.*"

BOOK TITLE
I'm Flying
AUTHOR
Alan Wade
ILLUSTRATOR
Petra Mathers
PUBLISHER
Alfred A. Knopf
PUBLICATION DATE
1990

ILLUSTRATION MEDIUM
Watercolor
PHOTOGRAPHER
Michael Mathers

"*I wanted the reader to feel the flight and the weather. The hero escapes from the suburbs, which are supposed to be boring. I wanted to show that they are also whacky, anyplace is. But if you've lived there too long, you might want to take off.*"

BOOK TITLE
Theodor and Mr. Balbini
AUTHOR
Petra Mathers
ILLUSTRATOR
Petra Mathers
PUBLISHER
HarperCollins
PUBLICATION DATE
1988
ILLUSTRATION MEDIUM
Watercolor
PHOTOGRAPHER
Michael Mathers

"*I never concern myself with the medium. Watercolor works for me. I am not interested in technique, I just want to tell the story. To me content is what counts. I wanted Mr. Balbini solid but suddenly in trouble with his tedious talking dog. At the same time, I wanted Theodor to be liked if only because all of us are Theodors too. There is someone for everyone. Theodor finds Madame Poulet who is gregarious, Mr. Balbini, who is quiet, finds Josephine who will be a quiet companion.*"

Gerald McDermott

Born in Detroit, Gerald McDermott began taking classes at the Detroit Institute of Art when he was four years old. He then attended Cass Technical High School where he was awarded a National Scholastic Scholarship to Pratt Institute. Once in New York, he began to produce and direct a series of animated films on mythology in consultation with Joseph Campbell. Since then, his artistic achievements include the Caldecott Medal for *Arrow to the Sun,* and a Caldecott Honor Award for *Anansi the Spider.* He also received the Silver Lion Award at the Venice Film Festival. His films have been shown at the Museum of Modern Art and the Whitney Museum in New York. Solo shows of his paintings and graphics have been held at the Everson Museum, Syracuse, the Children's Museum, Indianapolis, and are in the permanent collection of the Wichita Falls Museum of Art in Texas.

BOOK TITLE
Arrow to the Sun: A Pueblo Indian Tale
AUTHOR
Gerald McDermott
ILLUSTRATOR
Gerald McDermott
PUBLISHER
Viking Press
PUBLICATION DATE
1974
ILLUSTRATION MEDIUM
Gouache with collage

"*In* Arrow to the Sun, *my goal was to combine the power and boldness of traditional Pueblo arts with my own vision as a contemporary artist. The formal dignity of the masked dancers of Pueblo ritual, the rich earth colors of the high desert, the blazing intensity of the sun were all elements in forging the images of the book. All these elements are present in the painting of the Arrowmaker, the wise shaman who guides the hero on his journey.*"

The people celebrated his return in the
Dance of Life.

BOOK TITLE
Anansi the Spider: A Tale from the Ashanti
AUTHOR
Gerald McDermott
ILLUSTRATOR
Gerald McDermott
PUBLISHER
Holt, Rinehart & Winston
PUBLICATION DATE
1972
ILLUSTRATION MEDIUM
Pre-separated collage overlays

"*A*nansi the Spider *was my first picture book, and I adapted it from my own animated film. Although I had created over 4,000 drawings for the animation, all the art was rendered anew for the book. I wanted to retain the bold, graphic feeling of the film and carry over its visual rhythms to the printed page. This double-page spread exemplifies my approach, with the different 'stages' of Anansi's journey shown simultaneously.*"

BOOK TITLE
Tim O'Toole and the Wee Folk: An Irish Tale
AUTHOR
Gerald McDermott
ILLUSTRATOR
Gerald McDermott
PUBLISHER
Viking Kestrel
PUBLICATION DATE
1990
ILLUSTRATION MEDIUM
Colored pencil and transparent watercolor

"*I*t is my delight to discover a different visual style for each new project, and I used a more fully-rendered illustrational approach for the 19th-century Irish tale, Tim O'Toole and the Wee Folk. The gangly, tattered Tim and the green-suited leprechauns were drawn in detail with colored pencil on Bristol Board, then highlighted with a wash of transparent watercolors.*"

BOOK TITLE
**Zomo the Rabbit: A Trickster Tale
from West Africa**
AUTHOR
Gerald McDermott
ILLUSTRATOR
Gerald McDermott
PUBLISHER
Harcourt Brace Jovanovich
PUBLICATION DATE
1992
ILLUSTRATION MEDIUM
Gouache on watercolor paper

"Since Zomo the Rabbit is a classic 'trickster' character, I wanted him to leap off the page with an energy and vibrancy that reflect his origins in the lively oral tradition of West Africa. The mischievous rabbit, his animal adversaries, and the stylized landscape they inhabit are illustrated in broad blocks of intense color with a filigree of fine detail, just as the fabric designs of West Africa are rendered. As in all my work based on folktale and myth, I've sought to balance modern art and traditional folk design."

Charles Mikolaycak

Charles Mikolaycak was born in Scranton, Pennsylvania, in 1937. He received his B.F.A. from Pratt Institute and studied book design at New York University. Following a 13-year career at Time–Life Books, he left to devote himself entirely to children's book illustration. His first book, *Great Wolf and the Good Woodsman,* was published in 1967. Since then, he has illustrated over 60 children's books, including two ALA Notable Books, *How Wilka Went to Sea* in 1975, and *I Am Joseph* in 1980. *Babushka,* which he both wrote and illustrated, was among *The New York Times* Best Illustrated Children's Books for 1984. His work has appeared in numerous book shows of the American Institute of Graphic Arts, the Children's Book Showcase, and The Biennale of Illustration, Bratislava.

BOOK TITLE
Tam Lin
AUTHOR
Jane Yolen
ILLUSTRATOR
Charles Mikolaycak
PUBLISHER
Harcourt Brace Jovanovich
PUBLICATION DATE
1990
ILLUSTRATION MEDIUM
**Colored pencils and watercolor
on diazo print**

"*All my illustrations are done the same size as the printed book. For full-color books I always use pencils and watercolors. The drawings are carefully composed on many tissue overlays using set type in position. When a suitable solution to the problems in each spread of the book is reached, I then do a very finished pencil drawing on tissue. This drawing is then passed through an Ozalid printer providing me with a print in black or sepia line. (This process is also called diazo and is similar to the one architects use in making blueprints.) The print is then mounted on a smooth 3-ply Bristol Board and colored with colored pencils.*"

"*The challenge I encountered in this book was to design probable tartans for characters, working with two colors much mentioned in the text—red and green.*"

BOOK TITLE
Babushka
AUTHOR
Charles Mikolaycak
ILLUSTRATOR
Charles Mikolaycak

PUBLISHER
Holiday House
PUBLICATION DATE
1984
ILLUSTRATION MEDIUM
Colored pencil and watercolor on diazo print

"This was my retelling of a favorite story from my childhood. I wanted to evoke the mystery and magic I felt in looking at the illustrations from my childhood book. Those were more cartoon-like and schematic. I had to bring a greater sense of place and more richness to satisfy my grown-up sensibilities."

BOOK TITLE
The Legend of the Christmas Rose
AUTHOR
Selma Lagerlöf, retold by Ellin Greene
ILLUSTRATOR
Charles Mikolaycak
PUBLISHER
Holiday House
PUBLICATION DATE
1990
ILLUSTRATION MEDIUM
Colored pencils and watercolor on diazo print

"The challenge here was to give a reality to a rather sentimental tale, a look that would feel like the Northern setting—stark yet mysterious—of the title."

Wendell Minor

BOOK TITLE
Sierra
AUTHOR
Diane Siebert
ILLUSTRATOR
Wendell Minor
PUBLISHER
HarperCollins
PUBLICATION DATE
1991
ILLUSTRATION MEDIUM
Acrylic on masonite panels

The son of Norwegian and German heritage, Wendell Minor spent his childhood in Aurora, Illinois, and studied at the Ringling School of Art in Florida and the Kansas City Art Institute. The recipient of over 200 awards from every major graphics competition, he has received the Silver Medal from the New York Art Directors Club, over 50 Certificates of Merit in 15 Society of Illustrators Annual Exhibitions, and an Award of Excellence from the Fifty Books Show of the American Institute of Graphic Arts. Mr. Minor was chosen as one of a six-member team commissioned by NASA to capture the spirit of the Shuttle Discovery's Return to Flight in 1988, and in 1989 he designed the North Dakota Statehood Commemorative Stamp. Since 1978 he has been on the faculty of the School of Visual Arts, and for seven years he has served as president of the Society of Illustrators.

BOOK TITLE
Heartland
AUTHOR
Diane Siebert
ILLUSTRATOR
Wendell Minor
PUBLISHER
HarperCollins
PUBLICATION DATE
1989
ILLUSTRATION MEDIUM
Acrylic on masonite panels

"The paintings for Mojave, Heartland and Sierra were all painted in acrylic on gessoed masonite panels."

"These three books, with text by Diane Siebert, consist of poetry referring to the land in the first person."

"The land, therefore, speaks to children directly about nature and the environment. Each book brings a message to the reader that reinforces our concerns for preservation of the world for future generations."

"My paintings tell their own story of nature's beauty when the balance of nature is in harmony with all living things, including man."

BOOK TITLE
Mojave
AUTHOR
Diane Siebert
ILLUSTRATOR
Wendell Minor
PUBLISHER
HarperCollins
PUBLICATION DATE
1988
ILLUSTRATION MEDIUM
Acrylic on masonite panels

Beni Montresor

Born in Italy, Beni Montresor has received wide acclaim as a film and opera director, writer, and designer as well as illustrator of numerous children's books. Among his many honors and awards are the Caldecott Medal for *May I Bring a Friend?* by Beatrice Schenk de Regniers, and two *New York Times* Best Illustrated Children's Books. One of his most recent picture books, *The Witches of Venice,* is soon to be produced as a ballet with music by Philip Glass.

"Medium and style for these illustrations come out of my theater technique."

BOOK TITLE
Little Red Riding Hood
AUTHOR
Original story by
Charles Perrault
ILLUSTRATOR
Beni Montresor
PUBLISHER
Doubleday
PUBLICATION DATE
1991
ILLUSTRATION MEDIUM
Pencil drawing, re-worked by photocopy, pen ink added, re-worked by photocopy, resulting in a collage—using technology as part of the medium

Barry Moser

Born in Chattanooga, Tennessee, Barry Moser was educated at Auburn University, the University of Tennessee, and the University of Massachusetts at Amherst. He studied with George Cress, Leonard Baskin, and Jack Coughlin. Among his illustrated books are over 80 titles, including Lewis Carroll's *Alice's Adventures in Wonderland* which won the American Book Award for design and illustration. Mr. Moser has exhibited internationally in both one-man and group exhibits and is an associate of the National Academy of Design. In addition to being a designer, printer, painter, printmaker and illustrator, he frequently lectures and acts as visiting artist at universities and institutions across the country.

BOOK TITLE
Appalachia: The Voices of Sleeping Birds
AUTHOR
Cynthia Rylant
ILLUSTRATOR
Barry Moser
PUBLISHER
Pennyroyal Press, used with permission Harcourt Brace Jovanovich, San Diego
PUBLICATION DATE
1991
ILLUSTRATION MEDIUM
Wood engraving and transparent watercolor

BOOK TITLE
**Little Tricker the Squirrel Meets
Big Double the Bear**
AUTHOR
Ken Kesey
ILLUSTRATOR
Barry Moser

PUBLISHER
**Pennyroyal Press, used by
permission Viking Press
New York**
PUBLICATION DATE
1990
ILLUSTRATION MEDIUM
**Wood engraving and transparent
watercolor**

"As an artist of the book I see the book as a medium—the same as canvas and paint are to a painter, the same as wax and clay are to a sculptor, the same as harmony and timbre are to a composer. To me the illustrated book is the sum total of: first, a text; second, a design; third, typography; and finally (in fourth place) pictures. Because, you see, beautiful illustrations alone do not make beautiful books. For me the book is a unit—a whole."

"I begin my work by reading the text over and over—to the point of memorization. I then let it incubate for a while, listening for the stories to tell me...what kind of imagery would be both appropriate and provoking."

"*As for media, I prefer the demanding and unforgiving: wood engraving and transparent watercolor. The dark nature of engraving has influenced my typically dark watercolor palette and my sense of the 'presence' of the image on the page.*"

BOOK TITLE
Jump On Over!
AUTHOR
Joel Chandler Harris
Van Dyke Parks
ILLUSTRATOR
Barry Moser
PUBLISHER
Pennyroyal Press, used with permission Harcourt Brace Jovanovich, San Diego
PUBLICATION DATE
1989
ILLUSTRATION MEDIUM
Wood engraving and transparent watercolor

Roxie Munro

Photo: Bo Zaunders

BOOK TITLE
**The Inside-Outside Book of
New York City**
AUTHOR
Roxie Munro
ILLUSTRATOR
Roxie Munro
PUBLISHER
G.P. Putnam's Sons
PUBLICATION DATE
1985
ILLUSTRATION MEDIUM
**Ink and watercolor
(colored dyes)**

Author/illustrator Roxie Munro studied at the University of Maryland and Maryland Institute College of Art. In 1969 she earned a B.F.A. in painting at the University of Hawaii and then undertook graduate work at Ohio University and the University of Hawaii. Her work has been widely exhibited throughout the U.S. and Europe, including solo shows in Baltimore, Delaware, Washington and London. In 1985 she won *The New York Times* Best Illustrated Children's Books Award for *The Inside-Outside Book of New York City,* which also made the *Time Magazine* Best Children's Book List. Her work again received *The New York Times* Best Illustrated Children's Books Award in 1989 with the publication of *Blimps.*

"Since childhood I've been fascinated with the way perspective shifts as you move through space. Cities are particularly good subject matter, with their complex streets and big buildings. I've also been madly curious about what happens behind all those city windows...what kinds of work goes on? What does it look like behind the scene?"

133

BOOK TITLE
The Inside-Outside Book of London
AUTHOR
Roxie Munro
ILLUSTRATOR
Roxie Munro
PUBLISHER
Dutton Children's Books
PUBLICATION DATE
1989
ILLUSTRATION MEDIUM
Ink and watercolor (colored inks)

"I love to travel, and went to London four times researching this book. As with the other Inside-Outside books (New York City, Washington, D.C., and Paris) I am interested in changing visual perceptions, seeing from a personal point-of-view things which we sometimes take for granted, or that we see so often we cannot observe with a fresh eye."

BOOK TITLE
Blimps
AUTHOR
Roxie Munro
ILLUSTRATOR
Roxie Munro
PUBLISHER
Dutton Children's Books
PUBLICATION DATE
1989
ILLUSTRATION MEDIUM
Ink and watercolor (colored inks)

"*The fun thing here was the research: I got a private 3-hour ride in a blimp over Manhattan, and in England visited the biggest blimp-making factory in the world. I am interested in how things are made, how they work, and also in flying (my father and brother are pilots) so this book linked them all together.*"

135

Keiko Narahashi

Photo: Peter Belamarich

Born in Tokyo, Keiko Narahashi moved to the U.S. at age six. Influenced by a wonderful childhood collection of Japanese and English picture books, she also found that studying piano for 15 years taught her to appreciate art—to internalize movement and feeling before expressing it in music or drawing. Educated at North Carolina School of the Arts, Oberlin College and Parsons School of Design, she began working on children's books in 1985 when she wrote and illustrated *I Have a Friend,* a book about shadows cast on a sunny day and very much an expression of the feelings and atmosphere of her own childhood. Keiko Narahashi views her work in children's book illustration as an endless source of joy.

BOOK TITLE
I Have a Friend
AUTHOR
Keiko Narahashi
ILLUSTRATOR
Keiko Narahashi
PUBLISHER
Margaret K. McElderry Books
PUBLICATION DATE
1987
ILLUSTRATION MEDIUM
Watercolor

"This was my first children's book and, so far, the only one that I have written. On the surface, it is about a child discovering his shadow, but I was also interested in what children think about and imagine when playing alone. I wanted a clean, uncluttered, sunlit look that would evoke a sense of how a child sees the world."

BOOK TITLE
Who Said Red?
AUTHOR
Mary Serfozo
ILLUSTRATOR
Keiko Narahashi
PUBLISHER
Margaret K. McElderry Books
PUBLICATION DATE
1988
ILLUSTRATION MEDIUM
Watercolor and gouache

"The text for Who Said Red? left so much up to the illustrator that coming up with the context and scenario turned out to be the most challenging part of the book. I worked in watercolor and gouache so I could get varying intensities of color saturation—important in a book about colors."

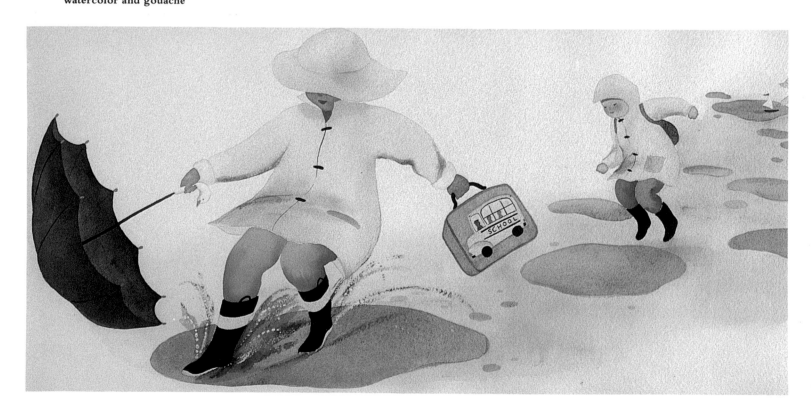

Jan Ormerod

Photo: Carole Cutner

Born in Western Australia in 1946, Jan Ormerod trained as a designer and an art teacher. In the late sixties she began teaching in high schools and then went on to the Art and Design Department of WAIT, where she lectured in drawing and design. Since the publication of her first book in 1981, Ms. Ormerod has become a leading children's book illustrator. Her work has been published in 14 countries, in languages as diverse as Chinese and Hebrew. She has won awards in America and Australia and in 1982 she won the Mother Goose Award for her illustrations in *Sunshine*. In 1986, *Happy Christmas, Gemma* was shortlisted for the Smarties Prize.

BOOK TITLE
Sunshine
AUTHOR
Jan Ormerod
ILLUSTRATOR
Jan Ormerod
PUBLISHER
Lothrop, Lee & Shepard
PUBLICATION DATE
1981
ILLUSTRATION MEDIUM
Line and inks

"*Illustrating a wordless book is like making a film, then choosing stills from that film to show the reader. By using comic strip convention for the layout of* Sunshine, *I was able to control the pace of the events, celebrating the independence of a small girl.*"

139

BOOK TITLE
Reading
AUTHOR
Jan Ormerod
ILLUSTRATOR
Jan Ormerod
PUBLISHER
Lothrop, Lee & Shepard
PUBLICATION DATE
1985
ILLUSTRATION MEDIUM
Pencil line and wash

"*This book looks at the loving relationship between a father and a crawling baby. I chose to use 'baby's eye view' and bring the adult down to floor level, squatting, kneeling, lying and crawling to fit the format—stretching my ingenuity and the model's patience to the limit. The black-and-white cat on each spread is used to focus attention on the relevant action, and to highlight any humorous moments.*"

BOOK TITLE
101 Things to Do with a Baby
AUTHOR
Jan Ormerod
ILLUSTRATOR
Jan Ormerod
PUBLISHER
Lothrop, Lee & Shepard
PUBLICATION DATE
1984
ILLUSTRATION MEDIUM
Black ink brush line and inks

"*I delighted in depicting the 101 ways my seven-year-old related to her baby sister. I chose brush line because of my admiration for Japanese prints. This created such difficulty with continuity, that I have never used that medium in a picture book again!*"

Nancy Winslow Parker

Photo: Artone Studio

BOOK TITLE
Frogs, Toads, Lizards, and Salamanders
AUTHOR
Nancy Winslow Parker and Joan Richards Wright
ILLUSTRATOR
Nancy Winslow Parker
PUBLISHER
Greenwillow Books
PUBLICATION DATE
1990
ILLUSTRATION MEDIUM
Ink line, colored pencils and watercolors

"In 1973, I said 'good-bye' to the work-a-day world of large corporations in New York City, where I had toiled for 20 years, and started anew as a writer and illustrator of children's books. My first book was *The Man with the Take-Apart Head,* published by Dodd Mead in 1973. Since then, I have explored crocodiles, hippopotami, cats, dogs, and Transylvanian Tree Toads; the U.S. Government and the United Nations. Sometimes people give me awards, like the two Christopher Medals which I cherish."

"*M*ainly to satisfy my own curiosity about the differences between frogs and toads, and the differences between lizards and salamanders, did my co-author and I decide to write Frogs, Toads, Lizards and Salamanders, a sequel to Bugs. The illustrations may have dictated the specimens selected as we wanted variety in size and coloration. This was easy for salamanders, lizards and frogs. Toads, on the other hand, look a lot like one another so wide geographical range was introduced in the selection process. The style of the 'scientific' drawings was to be a little less scientific than a college textbook, all the while retaining a cartoon-like overall feeling. In all modesty, I wish I had had a book like this when I studied Biology 101 in college.*"

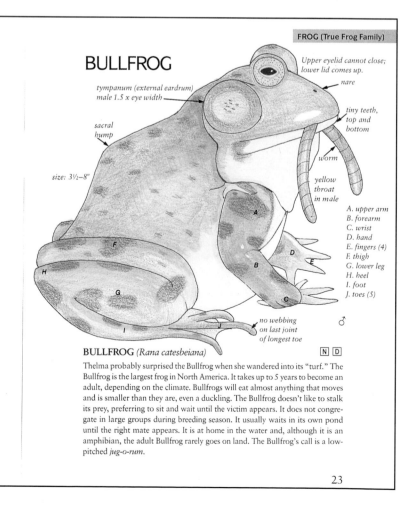

While picking berries near the bog, Thelma found a big Bullfrog.

FROG (True Frog Family)

BULLFROG

Upper eyelid cannot close; lower lid comes up.

tympanum (external eardrum) male 1.5 x eye width

nare

tiny teeth, top and bottom

sacral hump

worm

size: 3½–8"

yellow throat in male

A. upper arm
B. forearm
C. wrist
D. hand
E. fingers (4)
F. thigh
G. lower leg
H. heel
I. foot
J. toes (5)

no webbing on last joint of longest toe

♂

BULLFROG (*Rana catesbeiana*) ☒ ☒

Thelma probably surprised the Bullfrog when she wandered into its "turf." The Bullfrog is the largest frog in North America. It takes up to 5 years to become an adult, depending on the climate. Bullfrogs will eat almost anything that moves and is smaller than they are, even a duckling. The Bullfrog doesn't like to stalk its prey, preferring to sit and wait until the victim appears. It does not congregate in large groups during breeding season. It usually waits in its own pond until the right mate appears. It is at home in the water and, although it is an amphibian, the adult Bullfrog rarely goes on land. The Bullfrog's call is a low-pitched *jug-o-rum.*

22

23

BOOK TITLE
Bugs
AUTHOR
**Nancy Winslow Parker and
Joan Richards Wright**
ILLUSTRATOR
Nancy Winslow Parker
PUBLISHER
Greenwillow Books
PUBLICATION DATE
1987
ILLUSTRATION MEDIUM
**Ink line, colored pencils and
watercolors**

What bug bit Thelma on the thigh?

A horsefly.

HORSEFLY

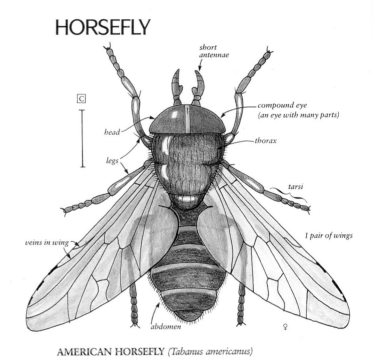

AMERICAN HORSEFLY *(Tabanus americanus)*

A hard-biting horsefly nipped Thelma. Horseflies live and breed near swamps and stagnant water. The male horsefly feeds on pollen and nectar, the female on blood. The female's bite bleeds longer than other insects' bites because her saliva contains a chemical that prevents blood clotting. The American Horsefly is found on the Atlantic seaboard and in the midwest from Texas to Canada's Northwest Territories. Flies are everywhere.

· 4 ·   · 5 ·

"The Bugs format underwent several metamorphoses until the final one emerged in the 16 examples finally selected. The double-page spread of one age level on the left and a higher age level on the right caused many sleepless nights—but, not to worry! The multi-age levels turned out to be an unexpected asset appealing to children of all ages and their parents. Nonfiction has limitless possibilities for invention. This book grew from a desire to show teeny tiny everyday bugs in giant size, like a greenhead fly as the beautifully created creature it is—antennae, tarsi, eyes, abdomens and all."

BOOK TITLE
My Mom Travels a Lot
AUTHOR
Caroline Feller Bauer
ILLUSTRATOR
Nancy Winslow Parker
PUBLISHER
Frederick Warne
PUBLICATION DATE
1981
ILLUSTRATION MEDIUM
Colored pencils and watercolors

"*Illustrating* My Mom Travels a Lot *came at a time when I had just lived through Mimi-Glady's second litter. The event was so intimate as it took place in my tiny apartment, that it became part of the sub-plot. The illustrations are patently personal—my own kitchen, whelping box, living room couch, chairs and lamp. The Edward Hopper painting on the wall I had just seen at the Whitney Museum. I never think about what my illustrations evoke in the reader—I think about what they evoke in me.*"

"*When the text called for 'an unmade bed,' I knew I could not ever draw rumpled sheets and blankets—ergo a hammock strung taut between two bed posts.*"

Robert Andrew Parker

A graduate of the school of the Art Institute of Chicago, Robert Andrew Parker has illustrated more than 40 children's books beginning with *Pop Corn & Ma Goodness* which won a Caldecott Honor Award in 1970. More recently, *The Dancing Skeleton* was designated a *New York Times* Best Illustrated Children's Book in 1989. Mr. Parker has taught at the School of Visual Arts, Parsons School of Design, Rhode Island School of Design and Pratt Institute. In 1969–1970 he was awarded a Guggenheim Fellowship. His work is represented in major private and public collections throughout the world, and he has also produced paintings and drawings for films, opera and theater sets.

BOOK TITLE
The Dancing Skeleton
AUTHOR
Cynthia DeFelice
ILLUSTRATOR
Robert Andrew Parker
PUBLISHER
Macmillan Publishing Co.
PUBLICATION DATE
1989
ILLUSTRATION MEDIUM
Watercolor

"I suppose the challenge of this book was to show in a light manner an essentially macabre story."

"*This book was a great pleasure to do. I liked the story. The period was my own childhood. I tried to fill it with images from 1940—a time I remember more easily than 1988.*"

BOOK TITLE
Randolph's Dream
AUTHOR
Judith Mellecker
ILLUSTRATOR
Robert Andrew Parker
PUBLISHER
Alfred A. Knopf
PUBLICATION DATE
1991
ILLUSTRATION MEDIUM
Watercolor

BOOK TITLE
Grandfather Tang's Story
AUTHOR
Ann Tompert
ILLUSTRATOR
Robert Andrew Parker
PUBLISHER
Crown Publishers Inc.
PUBLICATION DATE
1990
ILLUSTRATION MEDIUM
Watercolor

"The interesting thing about this book was researching Chinese life in the mid-eighteenth century and working with an art director who allowed complete freedom."

Brian Pinkney

Illustrator Brian Pinkney holds a B.F.A. from Philadelphia College of Art and a M.F.A. from the School of Visual Arts. His first picture book, *The Boy and the Ghost,* won the 1990 *Parents Choice* Honor Award for Illustration. *The Ballad of Belle Dorcas* won the 1990 *Parents Choice* Award for Story Books and received a certificate of Excellence from *Parenting* magazine. Mr. Pinkney's work has appeared in *The New York Times* and *Woman's Day, Business Tokyo, Ebony Man,* and *Instructor* magazines. Recent exhibitions of his work include the 1990 Original Art Show, and a solo exhibition at the School of Visual Arts. Other showings include The New York Public Library's Schomburg Center for Research in Black Culture and Philadelphia's Afro-American Historical and Cultural Museum. In 1990 Brian Pinkney received the National Arts Club Award of Distinction.

"I discovered scratchboard when I was getting my master's degree at the School of Visual Arts. I was going to do The Ballad of Belle Dorcas *in watercolor at first. Then, in the middle of the project, I asked to change to scratchboard. Working on scratchboard is like sculpting the image as well as drawing it. My work has a lot of energy and requires a sense of movement. I think scratchboard expresses this best."*

BOOK TITLE
The Ballad of Belle Dorcas
AUTHOR
William Hooks
ILLUSTRATOR
Brian Pinkney
PUBLISHER
Alfred A. Knopf
PUBLICATION DATE
1990
ILLUSTRATION MEDIUM
Scratchboard and watercolor

BOOK TITLE
Where Does the Trail Lead?
AUTHOR
Burton Albert
ILLUSTRATOR
Brian Pinkney

PUBLISHER
Simon & Schuster
PUBLICATION DATE
1991
ILLUSTRATION MEDIUM
Scratchboard and oil pastel

"*I liked researching this book. It took me back to my childhood at Cape Cod. Most of the images came through recreating experiences I had at the beach.*"

BOOK TITLE
The Boy and the Ghost
AUTHOR
Robert San Souci
ILLUSTRATOR
Brian Pinkney
PUBLISHER
Simon & Schuster
PUBLICATION DATE
1989
ILLUSTRATION MEDIUM
Pencil and watercolor

"*When I read* The Boy and the Ghost *I thought, 'That's me — that's me as a little boy.' And when I took the project and looked for a model, I looked for a little boy like me. The story is set in the South which interested me because I like projects that relate to my life, my heritage. I do research to find out more about myself, which is why I'm interested in Black projects. I want to be known as a Black artist because there's a need out there.*"

Jerry Pinkney

Born in Philadelphia in 1939, Jerry Pink-ney was educated at the Philadelphia College of Art where he was influenced by the classic illustrations of N.C. Wyeth and Howard Pyle. A winner of the Caldecott Honor Award for both *Mirandy and Brother Wind* and *The Talking Eggs,* he is also a three-time winner of the Coretta Scott King Award for Illustration. In 1989 his book *Turtle in July* was named a *New York Times* Best Illustrated Children's Book and was also among *Time* magazine's Twelve Outstanding Works for Children. Mr. Pinkney's illustrations have been exhibited in solo shows in galleries and museums throughout the U.S., including the Original Art Show in New York City. He has also designed numerous commemorative stamps for the U.S. Postal Service and has done artwork for *National Geographic, Essence Magazine,* IBM, the Negro Ensemble Company and NASA.

BOOK TITLE
The Talking Eggs
AUTHOR
Robert San Souci
ILLUSTRATOR
Jerry Pinkney
PUBLISHER
Dial Books for Young Readers
PUBLICATION DATE
1990
ILLUSTRATION MEDIUM
Pencil and watercolor on paper

"A good many of my children's books deal with the African American history and culture. The Talking Eggs manuscript provided me with a rich creole folktale from the American South. The story is full of fantasy, which I have always enjoyed illustrating. The story is in many ways the African American version of Cinderella."

BOOK TITLE
Mirandy and Brother Wind
AUTHOR
Patricia C. McKissack
ILLUSTRATOR
Jerry Pinkney

PUBLISHER
Alfred A. Knopf
PUBLICATION DATE
1989
ILLUSTRATION MEDIUM
Pencil and watercolor on paper

"*With* Mirandy and Brother Wind *I started the book in a small format. But once I got into working on the manuscript, I knew I needed much more space to tell the story visually. Mirandy is the kind of story where the landscape is important because I saw the wind as a dominant character. To give Brother Wind his proper place in the book, I needed a larger format.*"

BOOK TITLE
Turtle in July
AUTHOR
Marilyn Singer
ILLUSTRATOR
Jerry Pinkney
PUBLISHER
Macmillan Publishing Co.
PUBLICATION DATE
1990
ILLUSTRATION MEDIUM
**Pencil, watercolor, and colored
inks on paper**

"When I start a drawing I get as many pictures of the animal as possible. I begin working on a thumbnail sketch. I am trying at this point to work out the way I will later illustrate the animal. Will it be a close-up or a view from some distance? These are questions I ask myself. Most of the illustrations in Turtle In July are close-ups. My intent was to have the animals look out at the viewer, as if they were reciting the poem. If you read the poems, especially out loud, you can feel what I wanted to achieve. It was also important to me to have the animal look as natural as possible."

151

Patricia Polacco

Photo: Al Guiteras

Born in Lansing, Michigan, author/illustrator Patricia Polacco attended colleges and universities in California and Australia, completing a Ph.D. in Art History in 1978. She is a Fellow of the Royal Australian Art Historians and a former art director for Galleys, a publication serving illustrators and writers throughout the U.S. As president of her own corporation, Babushka, Inc., she is concerned with promoting the exchange of art and artists with the Soviet Union and is in partnership with the Avante Garde Children's Art School in Leningrad. Among her many awards for illustration are the California Commonwealth Award for best picture book in 1991 (Babushka's Doll), the International Reading Association Award for best picture book for young readers, and the Sydney Taylor Award from the Association of Jewish Librarians in 1989.

BOOK TITLE
The Keeping Quilt
AUTHOR
Patricia Polacco
ILLUSTRATOR
Patricia Polacco
PUBLISHER
Simon & Schuster
PUBLICATION DATE
1988
ILLUSTRATION MEDIUM
Pentel markers, acrylic paint, ink, pencil and oil pastel

"This book deals with the importance of family and keeping beliefs alive. Holding tradition and ritual as part of family gathering and talk. I still possess the keeping quilt—the oldest pieces on it are parts of Anna's dress and those pieces are about 110 years old. The quilt itself had to be rebacked and sewn about 50 years ago by my grandmother. I take it on school visits so that children can see it and touch it. From this, some of the children then make real quilts…they start a tradition of their own to pass on into the future."

BOOK TITLE
Babushka's Doll
AUTHOR
Patricia Polacco
ILLUSTRATOR
Patricia Polacco
PUBLISHER
Simon & Schuster
PUBLICATION DATE
1990
ILLUSTRATION MEDIUM
Pentel markers, acrylic paint, ink, pencil and oil pastel

BOOK TITLE
Thunder Cake
AUTHOR
Patricia Polacco
ILLUSTRATOR
Patricia Polacco
PUBLISHER
Philomel Books
PUBLICATION DATE
1990
ILLUSTRATION MEDIUM
**Pentel markers, acrylic paint,
ink, pencil and oil pastel**

"*If* I have any 'mission' at all in my writing and illustrations, it is to acquaint very young people with the magic of very old people. I know that my life certainly wouldn't have developed to what it is today had I not known my grandparents on both sides of my family. My father's people were 'shanty Irish,' plucky, humorous people steeped in folklore and good superstition. My mother's people were Russian jews from the Soviet Union, again magical folk that loved telling wondrous tales. I remember they took such delight in watching our faces when they unraveled a mystery of life before our eyes...I truly feel that old ones have a very special energy and can reach little ones because of their common interests in very basic things of life."

"I hope that my stories lead a younger person to wonder about magic. To believe, if you will, that magic is a reality and what they believe as a child is the most important formation of their imagery for the rest of their lives. Old folks have a very basic understanding in the importance of being able to dream and they share this with children."

BOOK TITLE
Rechenka's Eggs
AUTHOR
Patricia Polacco
ILLUSTRATOR
Patricia Polacco
PUBLISHER
Philomel Books
PUBLICATION DATE
1988
ILLUSTRATION MEDIUM
**Pentel markers, acrylic paint,
ink, pencil and oil pastel**

Photo: © 1979 Hilary Masters

Alice Provensen
Martin Provensen *(1916–1987)*

Alice Provensen and her late husband Martin published their first book together in 1947 and continued writing and illustrating books together for over 30 years. Among their widely-known books are *A Peaceable Kingdom, The Golden Serpent* and four books based on their experiences at Maple Hill Farm, their home in Dutchess County, New York. In 1984 they were awarded the Caldecott Medal for their illustrations in *The Glorious Flight.* The Provensens have been honored by the Art Books for Children Citation of the Brooklyn Museum, by the Gold Medal for Illustration of the Society of Illustrators, and by being included in *The New York Times* Best Illustrated Children's Books of the Year list on nine occasions.

BOOK TITLE
The Glorious Flight
AUTHORS
Alice and Martin Provensen
ILLUSTRATORS
Alice and Martin Provensen
PUBLISHER
The Viking Press
PUBLICATION DATE
1983
ILLUSTRATION MEDIUM
**Acrylic and ink on
illustration board**

"*Martin was obsessed with flying. I shared his interest in early flying machines. The excitement we both felt when actually aloft in these antique planes must have come across in* The Glorious Flight. *It won the Caldecott Medal for us.*"

This inn belongs to William Blake
and many are the beasts he's tamed
and many are the stars he's named
and many those who stop and take
their joyful rest with William Blake.

Two mighty dragons brew and bake
and many are the loaves they've burned
and many are the spits they've turned
and many those who stop and break
their joyful bread with William Blake.

Two patient angels wash and shake
his featherbeds, and far away
snow falls like feathers. That's the day
good children run outside and make
snowmen to honor William Blake.

14

"A Visit to William Blake's Inn by Nancy Willard was the first book of poetry to win the Newbery Medal. It was also a Caldecott Honor Book for illustration. It was the first children's book to carry two award stickers on its jacket."

BOOK TITLE
A Visit to William Blake's Inn
AUTHOR
Nancy Willard
ILLUSTRATORS
Alice and Martin Provensen
PUBLISHER
Harcourt Brace Jovanovich
PUBLICATION DATE
1981
ILLUSTRATION MEDIUM
**Acrylic and ink on
illustration board**

THEODORE ROOSEVELT

SAN FRANCISCO EARTHQUAKE 1906

ELLI 18

THE U.S. RECLAMATION ACT 1902

"NO MAN HAS LED A HAPPIER LIFE THAN I HAVE LED...A HAPPIER LIFE IN EVERY WAY."

NOBEL PEACE PRIZE FOR MEDIATING RUSSO-JAPANESE WAR 1906

1,000,000 IMMIGRANTS A YEAR

1902- ORIEN

1901-
1909

THE WRIGHT BROTHERS
FLY THE FIRST POWERED AIRCRAFT
AT KITTY HAWK, N.C. DECEMBER 17,
1903

INVENTION OF THE TEDDY BEAR

ALICE LEE · THEODORE · QUENTIN

KERMIT · ETHEL · ARCHIBALD

PANAMA
CANAL ZONE
ACQUIRED
1904

OKLAHOMA 1907 ADMITTED AS THE 46TH STATE

...LAND ...54

...EEK A NEW LIFE IN AMERICA

FIRST WIRELESS SIGNAL FROM ENGLAND

MARCONI'S

TO NEWFOUNDLAND 1901

...CLUSION 1907
...TENDED

BOOK TITLE
The Buck Stops Here
AUTHOR
Alice Provensen
ILLUSTRATOR
Alice Provensen
PUBLISHER
HarperCollins
PUBLICATION DATE
1990
ILLUSTRATION MEDIUM
Oil and ink on vellum

"The Buck Stops Here *was the first book I did by myself after Martin's death. My absorbing interest in American History, the amount of research required and the necessary sensitivity to the portraits and the politics of the book saw me through the most difficult period of my life.*"

"*The design problem in illustrating a chronology of U.S. presidents was to show the same man twice without confusing the terms of office. Cleveland's portraits are separated by that of Harrison who defeated Cleveland in 1889, only to have him re-elected in 1893.*"

157

Ted Rand

A native of the Pacific Northwest, Ted Rand was born in Seattle where he has taught illustration for 22 years at the University of Washington. His goal as an illustrator of children's books is to make the pictures and story inseparable—"so interlocked in fulfilling the total unity that they remain as one in the reader's mind." He allows the story to suggest the method of technical solution rather than trying to impose a style on the story. Ted Rand's children's illustrations are currently in print for nine different publishers. In 1991 he received the Christopher Medal for *Paul Revere's Ride*.

"The familiar poem, for an artist who works realistically, took considerable research. Paul Revere's biography provided factual background material. Watercolor was ideal for the night settings, and the kind of detail necessary to show the architecture and costumes of the period. I found portraits of Paul Revere to work from. I have walked the freedom trail in Boston, talked to the curator of the Old North Church, and used the Boston Public Library, all of which contributed importantly to the project."

"In designing the book, pacing was crucial to the movement of the story, and controls the pictorial order and subject matter."

BOOK TITLE
Paul Revere's Ride
AUTHOR
Longfellow
ILLUSTRATOR
Ted Rand
PUBLISHER
Dutton Children's Books
PUBLICATION DATE
1990
ILLUSTRATION MEDIUM
Transparent watercolor

158

BOOK TITLE
Country Crossing
AUTHOR
Jim Aylesworth
ILLUSTRATOR
Ted Rand
PUBLISHER
Atheneum
PUBLICATION DATE
1991
ILLUSTRATION MEDIUM
Sumi brush and chalk

BOOK TITLE
Salty Dog
AUTHOR
Gloria Rand
ILLUSTRATOR
Ted Rand

PUBLISHER
Henry Holt and Co., Inc.
PUBLICATION DATE
1989
ILLUSTRATION MEDIUM
Transparent watercolor and liquid dye color

"*The story takes place at night, a mood piece about a train heard in the distance, then roaring to a crossing, where an old car is stopped and waiting for the train to pass. The story begins quietly and ends in quiet. I chose sumi brush and chalk because the sumi brush, loaded with India ink can be used to great advantage in night scenes, and in representing the speeding train. Chalk can be rubbed and shaded to dramatize the night and speed. My objective was to show the change from quiet to the immediacy of a freight train, roaring past at close range, and then the return to the quiet night.*"

"*I chose traditional watercolor combined with the brilliance of Dr. Martin's liquid color because of the range of scenes, from interior to exterior, with the need for muted and for very bright colors.*"

"*The real find for reference was a boatbuilder, in the San Juan Islands, whose boatshed I used for the boat construction spreads. I also found the boat under construction in two different stages, so that I was able to show, with absolute accuracy, the construction of a wooden sailboat. This is typical of the kind of research I do wherever necessary. If I don't know the subject, I have learned to go to sources that can supply what I need to know.*"

Robert Rayevsky

Photo: Pien Kranenburg

BOOK TITLE
**Androcles and the Lion and
Other Aesop's Fables**
AUTHOR
Tom Paxton
ILLUSTRATOR
Robert Rayevsky
PUBLISHER
Morrow Junior Books
PUBLICATION DATE
1991
ILLUSTRATION MEDIUM
Pen and ink, watercolor, acrylics

Born and educated in Moscow, Robert Rayevsky emigrated to the U.S. in 1979 where he supported himself as a waiter and taxi driver while completing a B.F.A. at Parsons School of Design. Since the publication of his first children's book in 1985, he has illustrated 11 books. *Belling the Cat,* 1990, was cited among "Notable Children's Trade Books in the Field of Social Studies," and *Aesop's Fables,* 1988, was named one of the *School Library Journal's* Best Books of the Year. Mr. Rayevsky's art was reviewed in "1988 New York Art Review," an illustrated survey of the city's museums, galleries and leading artists.

Robert Rayevsky. 88

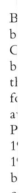

BOOK TITLE	PUBLISHER
Acsop's Fables	**Morrow Junior Books**
AUTHOR	PUBLICATION DATE
Tom Paxton	**1988**
ILLUSTRATOR	ILLUSTRATION MEDIUM
Robert Rayevsky	**Pen and ink, watercolor**

"*The Renaissance is the setting for these fables. The book is conceived as a theatrical staging, and the characters look like actors or dancers. In my work I wanted to repeat the simplicity and easiness of Tom Paxton's verses. I wanted the morals of Aesop's fables to be shown not through the reprimand, but through the illustrations which are rich in humor and details.*"

"*This is the third book of Aesop's Fables I have done in collaboration with Tom Paxton. In a series it is difficult to escape repeating oneself, not to use what has already been successful. At the same time there must be a link between all the books in a series. I have tried to maintain this link through the design while varying the illustrations in style and technique.*"

"*I also wanted to accent the point that Aesop's Fables are as relevant and close to us as they were to Aesop's contemporaries. Therefore, the first fable takes place in ancient Greece, the last—in contemporary New York.*"

BOOK TITLE
Effie
AUTHOR
Beverley Allinson
ILLUSTRATOR
Barbara Reid
PUBLISHER
Scholastic Canada Ltd.
PUBLICATION DATE
1990
ILLUSTRATION MEDIUM
Plasticine

"*From the first reading of the manuscript I knew Effie was going to be a lot of fun and a lot of work. I love clay animation and I felt that was a good look for this story full of silly characters and a lot of action. To solve some of the problems posed by a bug's eye view of the world, I used glaze, bits of string and brush bristles with the plasticine to get the look I wanted.*"

Glen Rounds

Born in 1906 in western South Dakota, Glen Rounds lived on a ranch in Montana until 1920. He attended the Kansas City Art Institute, worked in sign shops creating silk screen posters, and in 1930 attended the Art Students League in New York City. He painted signs and murals for speakeasies and began experimenting with etching, engraving and woodcuts. In 1935 he wrote his first children's book, *Ol' Paul the Mighty Logger,* which is still in print.

BOOK TITLE
Old MacDonald Had a Farm
ILLUSTRATOR
Glen Rounds
PUBLISHER
Holiday House
PUBLICATION DATE
1989
ILLUSTRATION MEDIUM
Brush and oil pastel

"This was an experiment—trying to equal the use of color and white space I still remember seeing in picture book lithographs 80 years ago."

BOOK TITLE
Wash Day on Noah's Ark
AUTHOR
Glen Rounds
ILLUSTRATOR
Glen Rounds
PUBLISHER
Holiday House
PUBLICATION DATE
1985
ILLUSTRATION MEDIUM
Pen and Conte chalk

"Here I wanted to counter the 'Tall Tale' treatment of the old story by giving the drawing careful weight and balance—a Rounds version of the old Sunday School cards. This was the first book I illustrated after being forced to draw with my left hand."

BOOK TITLE
**Mr. Yowder and the Lion
Roar Capsules**
AUTHOR
Glen Rounds
ILLUSTRATOR
Glen Rounds
PUBLISHER
Holiday House
PUBLICATION DATE
1976
ILLUSTRATION MEDIUM
Ink and brush

*"This is one of a series of 'Tall Tales' of the kind old uncles, cowboys
and such folk told young boys and gullible strangers."*

*"To keep the raffish, unshaven feeling of the sign painter I used the
scraggly brush line."*

Marisabina Russo

A graduate of Mount Holyoke College with a major in studio art, Marisabina Russo studied lithography at the Boston Museum School and life drawing at the Art Students League. She began her career in illustration working for newspapers and magazines and created several covers for *The New Yorker.* Her illustrations for *More Classic Italian Cooking* won a certificate of excellence from A.I.G.A. in 1978. After meeting Susan Hirschman in 1985 she began writing and illustrating her own picture books. Her work has recently been exhibited in New York ("Picture This..."), Japan ("Exhibition: Picture Books"), and Czechoslovakia (Bratislava International). Her illustrations for *The Line Up Book* won the International Reading Association Award for Best Picture Book.

BOOK TITLE
Waiting for Hannah
AUTHOR
Marisabina Russo
ILLUSTRATOR
Marisabina Russo
PUBLISHER
Greenwillow Books
PUBLICATION DATE
1989
ILLUSTRATION MEDIUM
Gouache on paper

"*I fall into the same pattern with each book: first I write the story in longhand. Usually I have to write and rewrite and change things several times but in this case I sat down, wrote it out, purely from the heart as a love poem to my daughter. I didn't even think it was really a picture book. In fact, I hid it under a pad for a few weeks before I got the nerve to send it to Susan Hirschman.*"

"*After I have the manuscript I begin preparing the dummy. First I do thumbnail sketches to help me figure out how I want to break up the text. Then I do a full size pencil dummy. The dummy is the hardest part of all because it is the underpinning of the whole book—the skeleton.*"

"*After the dummy is done, I begin the finished pictures. Pencil sketches on heavy watercolor paper and then I paint with gouache. This is my happiest time. I have done every book using the same media.*"

"*In this book I wanted the pictures to give the sense of time passing and of expectation, of how much the parents were looking forward to this baby.*"

BOOK TITLE
A Visit to Oma
AUTHOR
Marisabina Russo
ILLUSTRATOR
Marisabina Russo
PUBLISHER
Greenwillow Books
PUBLICATION DATE
1991
ILLUSTRATION MEDIUM
Gouache on paper

"For this book I did some research on the villages in Poland at the turn of the century for that is where I envisioned Oma's home. Again I had to show a difference between reality and Celeste's imagination. I particularly wanted to emphasize the warm relationship between the great-grandmother and the child despite the age difference and cultural differences. This had to be shown through facial expression and body language. I hoped this book would encourage other children to talk about family history and stories and realize how unique each one is. I spoke to a second grade class of E.S.L. students from many different Spanish speaking countries. Of all my books, they loved this one the best. Most of them come from extended families and have strong relationships with grandparents."

BOOK TITLE
A Visit to Oma
AUTHOR
Marisabina Russo
ILLUSTRATOR
Marisabina Russo
PUBLISHER
Greenwillow Books
PUBLICATION DATE
1991
ILLUSTRATION MEDIUM
Gouache on paper

"*For this book I did some research on the villages in Poland at the turn of the century for that is where I envisioned Oma's home. Again I had to show a difference between reality and Celeste's imagination. I particularly wanted to emphasize the warm relationship between the great-grandmother and the child despite the age difference and cultural differences. This had to be shown through facial expression and body language. I hoped this book would encourage other children to talk about family history and stories and realize how unique each one is. I spoke to a second grade class of E.S.L. students from many different Spanish speaking countries. Of all my books, they loved this one the best. Most of them come from extended families and have strong relationships with grandparents.*"

Marisabina Russo

A graduate of Mount Holyoke College with a major in studio art, Marisabina Russo studied lithography at the Boston Museum School and life drawing at the Art Students League. She began her career in illustration working for newspapers and magazines and created several covers for *The New Yorker*. Her illustrations for *More Classic Italian Cooking* won a certificate of excellence from A.I.G.A. in 1978. After meeting Susan Hirschman in 1985 she began writing and illustrating her own picture books. Her work has recently been exhibited in New York ("Picture This..."), Japan ("Exhibition: Picture Books"), and Czechoslovakia (Bratislava International). Her illustrations for *The Line Up Book* won the International Reading Association Award for Best Picture Book.

BOOK TITLE
Waiting for Hannah
AUTHOR
Marisabina Russo
ILLUSTRATOR
Marisabina Russo
PUBLISHER
Greenwillow Books
PUBLICATION DATE
1989
ILLUSTRATION MEDIUM
Gouache on paper

"*I fall into the same pattern with each book: first I write the story in longhand. Usually I have to write and rewrite and change things several times but in this case I sat down, wrote it out, purely from the heart as a love poem to my daughter. I didn't even think it was really a picture book. In fact, I hid it under a pad for a few weeks before I got the nerve to send it to Susan Hirschman.*"

"*After I have the manuscript I begin preparing the dummy. First I do thumbnail sketches to help me figure out how I want to break up the text. Then I do a full size pencil dummy. The dummy is the hardest part of all because it is the underpinning of the whole book—the skeleton.*"

"*After the dummy is done, I begin the finished pictures. Pencil sketches on heavy watercolor paper and then I paint with gouache. This is my happiest time. I have done every book using the same media.*"

"*In this book I wanted the pictures to give the sense of time passing and of expectation, of how much the parents were looking forward to this baby.*"

Uri Shulevitz

Uri Shulevitz is author and illustrator of over 29 books for children including: *One Monday Morning; Rain, Rain, Rivers; The Magician; Dawn;* and *The Treasure.* Among his many awards are the Caldecott Medal in 1969 for *The Fool of the World and The Flying Ship* and a Caldecott Honor Award for *The Treasure* in 1979. *Dawn* was chosen to represent the United States on the International Honors List at the 1976 International Board of Books for Young People Congress. Mr. Shulevitz is a member of the Children's Books Committee of the Author's Guild and is the author of *Writing with Pictures,* published in 1985.

BOOK TITLE
Toddlecreek Post Office
AUTHOR
Uri Shulevitz
ILLUSTRATOR
Uri Shulevitz
PUBLISHER
Farrar, Straus & Giroux
PUBLICATION DATE
1990
ILLUSTRATION MEDIUM
Watercolor

"*My* approach here has been to achieve a somewhat geometric, sculptural, chiseled effect in depicting people, animals, and settings. I wished to depict the main setting—the post office interior—as a theatre stage, in which the lighting—blue shadows and yellow sunlight—are equal participants in the unfolding drama of the story."

BOOK TITLE
**The Fool of the World
and the Flying Ship**
AUTHOR
**Folk tale retold by
Arthur Ransome**
ILLUSTRATOR
Uri Shulevitz
PUBLISHER
Farrar, Straus & Giroux
PUBLICATION DATE
1968
ILLUSTRATION MEDIUM
**Watercolor, colored inks, pen and
ink hatching**

"I wished to suggest large scale vistas, so typical of the large expanses of the flat landscapes of Russia. To combine, where story calls for, empty, large spaces with crowded scenes, and have the flying ship roaming through open skies. That is why I left the skies white."

BOOK TITLE
The Treasure
AUTHOR
Uri Shulevitz
ILLUSTRATOR
Uri Shulevitz
PUBLISHER
Farrar, Straus & Giroux
PUBLICATION DATE
1978
ILLUSTRATION MEDIUM
**Watercolor, retouched with
black lines**

"*I wished to combine intimate size pictures, that sometimes depict closed-in spaces, with open panoramic views. I used a variety of stages of the hero's journey. I've used atmospheric, misty backgrounds in the distance, to achieve an overall, somewhat soft effect.*"

Peter Sis

BOOK TITLE
The Midnight Horse
AUTHOR
Sid Fleischman
ILLUSTRATOR
Peter Sis
PUBLISHER
Greenwillow Books
PUBLICATION DATE
1990
ILLUSTRATION MEDIUM
Ink

The son of a filmmaker, Peter Sis grew up in Prague, Czechoslovakia, also known as "the city of a hundred towers," and the home of many stories, myths and legends. His parents and friends encouraged his artistic talents from an early age and he attended several art schools. Studying under Quentin Blake at London's Royal College of Art he came to realize that he wanted to illustrate his own stories and turn them into animated films. After illustrating his first book, *Bean Boy,* he moved to the United States and since then has illustrated 16 books. *The Whipping Boy* won the Newbery Medal in 1987 and *Rainbow Rhino* was named a *New York Times* Best Illustrated Book.

"Here I used the same approach as in a previous collaboration with the author. The colorful language lends itself to the almost grotesque visualization. I love to work on these books—they remind me of childhood summer vacations reading Jules Verne, Dickens and Twain (all those engraved illustrations with captions!) in the attic of my grandparents' house. I have tried to replace dots with lines to gain more texture and save some time—to no avail."

BOOK TITLE
Rainbow Rhino
AUTHOR
Peter Sis
ILLUSTRATOR
Peter Sis
PUBLISHER
Alfred A. Knopf
PUBLICATION DATE
1987
ILLUSTRATION MEDIUM
Oil

"*My* first book as an author, this story is based on what I like to paint (landscape, strange animals). It is also about feelings about coming from another country and culture and about friendship and harmony. The original idea was very complicated. Frances Foster worked on the basic pretext with me and made it work."

BOOK TITLE
Follow the Dream
AUTHOR
Peter Sis
ILLUSTRATOR
Peter Sis
PUBLISHER
Alfred A. Knopf
PUBLICATION DATE
1991
ILLUSTRATION MEDIUM
Oil, mixed media

"This book evolved from ideas about explorers and daring and per-suasion; it's about believing in one's dreams. I was trying to imagine a differ-ent time and different perspective of the 'world' and 'history.' I was also trying to imagine the journey—day after day without the common knowl-edge of Columbus's landing on October 10, 1492. This is my best work so far."

BOOK TITLE
Going Up!
AUTHOR
Peter Sis
ILLUSTRATOR
Peter Sis
PUBLISHER
Greenwillow Books
PUBLICATION DATE
1989
ILLUSTRATION MEDIUM
Color inks

"While thinking about the 'big' and 'painterly' ideas I have encoun-tered many little, funny, mostly urban observations—like waving (for a cab), going up (elevators in New York with all kinds of characters), and beach balls (beaches and all kinds of characters). Thanks to Susan Hirschman they be-came counting and coloring books—sort of cheerful messages from the big city. I have tried to simplify and color my academic style and I am proud of it. If I don't experiment now, then when?"

Lane Smith

Author/illustrator Lane Smith was born in Tulsa, Oklahoma, and earned a B.F.A. from Art Center College of Design in Pasadena in 1983. In addition to children's books, his work has appeared on numerous magazine covers and in newspapers worldwide. He has won three Silver Medals from The Society of Illustrators and his work has been included in several American Illustration Annuals. His book *Halloween ABC* was named a *New York Times* Best Illustrated Book in 1987 and was also selected by *School Library Journal* as a Best Book of the Year. Lane Smith's illustrations for *The Big Pets* won the Golden Apple Award at the Biennale in Bratislava in 1991.

BOOK TITLE
Halloween ABC
AUTHOR
Eve Merriam
ILLUSTRATOR
Lane Smith
PUBLISHER
Macmillan Publishing Co.
PUBLICATION DATE
1987
ILLUSTRATION MEDIUM
Oil

"Each page in this book showcased a letter of the alphabet. The challenge then, was one of composition. How to illustrate an image and have it not clash with the letterforms. I chose to do every image in the book as a central one...symmetrical. I wanted the picture to be an instant read... graphic, yet still incorporating my usual textures and techniques."

"I think the book turned out elegant and bold but still very spooky. I was tired of all the cute Halloween books. Halloween should be scary and fun."

BOOK TITLE
**The True Story of the
3 Little Pigs!**
AUTHOR
Jon Scieszka
ILLUSTRATOR
Lane Smith
PUBLISHER
Viking Penguin
PUBLICATION DATE
1989
ILLUSTRATION MEDIUM
Oil/mixed

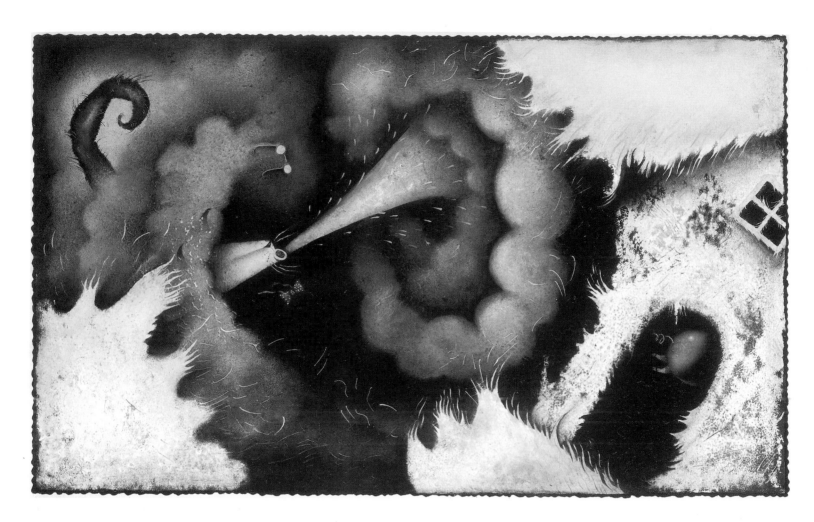

"*This story was very witty and funny. If I had gone too light with the colors, for instance, pen and ink washes, it could have made the humor a little too comical. Jon and I didn't want a goofy book.*"

"*The big challenge for me was how to show the pigs because the wolf actually eats them. If I showed them as sympathetic characters, the story would be too much for kids. So I only showed parts of them...like a pig rump which looks very similar to a ham. I portrayed the pigs always as 'food.' On the other hand, I gave the wolf an innocent look—glasses, bow-tie, etc.*"

"*I collaged real elements into the paintings (sticks, newspaper bits) to give them a dimensional look.*"

THE TRUE STORY OF THE 3 LITTLE PIGS!

BY A. WOLF

AS TOLD TO JON SCIESZKA
ILLUSTRATED BY LANE SMITH

BOOK TITLE
The Big Pets
AUTHOR
Lane Smith
ILLUSTRATOR
Lane Smith
PUBLISHER
Viking Penguin
PUBLICATION DATE
1991
ILLUSTRATION MEDIUM
Oil

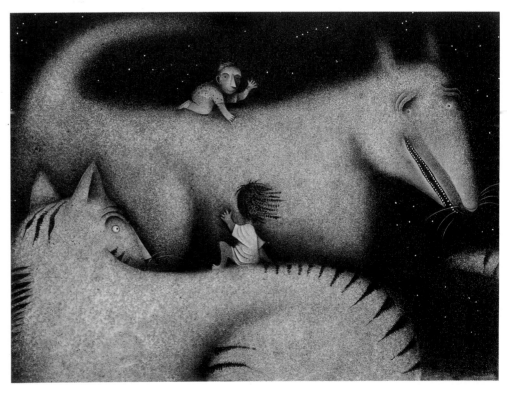

"*When I was a child I loved the mystery and security of night. I didn't see it as something unknown or frightening. I liked all the colored lights of the city. I liked hearing the wind blow the trees against the outside of my window. I imagined unexplored lands and adventures.*"

"*I reached back to my memories and brought them out for this book…a surreal, dream ride. The colors had to be dark and rich. I didn't want dialogue to clutter the experience. I wanted it to unfold like an 'amusement park' ride building to the 'Milky Way' climax.*"

Diane Stanley

BOOK TITLE
Good Queen Bess
AUTHOR
Diane Stanley and Peter Vennema
ILLUSTRATOR
Diane Stanley
PUBLISHER
Four Winds Press
PUBLICATION DATE
1990
ILLUSTRATION MEDIUM
Gouache

Author/illustrator Diane Stanley has published over 25 books for children. She earned a B.A. in history from Trinity University and an M.A. in medical illustration from Johns Hopkins University, working as a medical illustrator for several years before beginning a career in children's books. She has also worked as a designer and art director. Her award-winning books include *Good Queen Bess, Peter the Great,* both ALA Notable books, and *Shaka: King of the Zulus,* selected as a *New York Times* Best Illustrated Children's Book in 1988.

"The marvelous work of Elizabethan painters and the wonderful costumes of the age were my greatest inspiration in doing the illustrations. Because the paintings were so elaborate, I kept the design at its simplest. The art, like the age, has a formal quality (in contrast to the intimacy of The Last Princess)."

197

BOOK TITLE
Shaka: King of the Zulus
AUTHOR
Diane Stanley and Peter Vennema
ILLUSTRATOR
Diane Stanley
PUBLISHER
Morrow Junior Books
PUBLICATION DATE
1988
ILLUSTRATION MEDIUM
Gouache

"This book was extraordinarily hard to illustrate accurately, since Zulus in Shaka's time were not well documented. He was not painted from life and the details of costume had to be ferreted out from written descriptions."

"I used the Zulu beadwork as a design motif throughout and used a screen of yellow on the pages to bring up the warmth and color of Africa."

BOOK TITLE
The Last Princess
AUTHOR
Fay Stanley
ILLUSTRATOR
Diane Stanley
PUBLISHER
Four Winds Press
PUBLICATION DATE
1991
ILLUSTRATION MEDIUM
Gouache

"This story of a Hawaiian princess needed to reflect the lush, tropical beauty of Hawaii and contrast it with the cool greys of England. Gouache was the perfect medium to get the intense and brilliant colors I wanted for this book. I was inspired, in an indirect sort of way, by the paintings of Gauguin—especially in the colors."

"I spent some time in Indonesia while I was working on this book and I think what I saw there is reflected in the art. Also, because Kaiulani is a late-nineteenth-century figure, I had ample photographs to work from, a rich and wonderful source. This helped make it more intimate than my other biographies."

John Steptoe
(1950–1989)

Photo: James Ropiequet Schmidt

BOOK TITLE
The Story of Jumping Mouse
AUTHOR
Retold by John Steptoe
ILLUSTRATOR
John Steptoe
PUBLISHER
Lothrop, Lee & Shepard Books
PUBLICATION DATE
1984
ILLUSTRATION MEDIUM
Pencil and graphite

"*In* The Story of Jumping Mouse, *the gray of the pencil and the pencil itself became dominant. I didn't set out to do a black and white book, but as I developed the sketches, my understanding of light and dark was getting stronger and stronger. I'm challenged now by the problems of maintaining the sensitivity of black and white while using bright, strong colors. I want both of these elements—the sensitivity and the strong color—to balance in my paintings.*"

(Interview with John Steptoe published in *Library Talk,* September/October, 1988)

Award-winning author/illustrator John Steptoe grew up in the Bedford-Stuyvesant section of Brooklyn, attended the New York High School of Art and Design and published his first book, *Stevie,* at age 19. Dedicated to the creation of books for African American children, Steptoe went on to create *Mother Crocodile* (1982) and *Mufaro's Beautiful Daughters* (1988), both winners of numerous awards, including the Coretta Scott King Award for Illustration. *Mufaro's Beautiful Daughters* also received the *Boston Globe-Horn Book* Award and was named a Caldecott Honor Book. Through his portrayal of the lives and experiences of black children, John Steptoe wanted to share his conviction that African Americans have a reason to be proud.

BOOK TITLE
Mufaro's Beautiful Daughters
AUTHOR
John Steptoe
ILLUSTRATOR
John Steptoe
PUBLISHER
Lothrop, Lee & Shepard Books
PUBLICATION DATE
1987
ILLUSTRATION MEDIUM
Colored ink, watercolor and pencil

"*With* Mufaro's Beautiful Daughters, *I brought back the color. I added the old knowledge of coloration to my new discoveries of light and dark…I am very proud of* Mufaro's Beautiful Daughters. *In it I can see what is familiar to me. I can see the beauty of the people that I live with as well as the beauty of my past. Hopefully others can share this with me. It is a more truthful picture of myself. It says I am intelligent and beautiful.*"

(Handwritten material in John Steptoe Collection, the Schomberg Center for Research in Black Culture, New York City.)

BOOK TITLE
Mother Crocodile
AUTHOR
**Translated and adapted by
Rosa Guy**
ILLUSTRATOR
John Steptoe
PUBLISHER
Delacorte Press
PUBLICATION DATE
1981
ILLUSTRATION MEDIUM
Watercolors

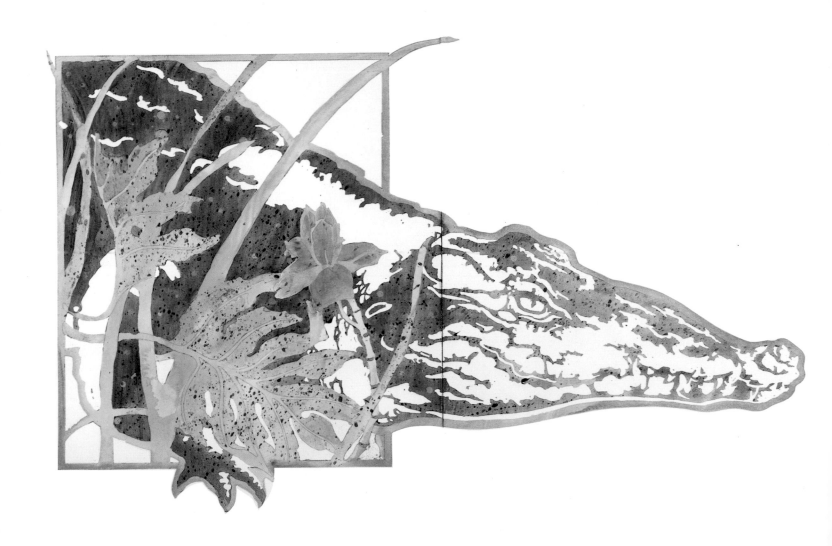

*"I've learned that it is always best to deal with the feelings of a story.
I'm sure that the illustrations in* Mother Crocodile *work because I tried to
deal with the emotional sense of this beautifully written book...Of course
I'm gratified sometimes by the positive social effect my work may have had.
But an effect comes after the aesthetic statement."*
(Acceptance Speech, Coretta Scott King Award, 1982)

Nancy Tafuri

Photo: Thomas Tafuri

Nancy Tafuri studied at the School of Visual Arts where she prepared for a graphics-related career. With her husband Tom she founded a graphic design studio dealing with book jacket design, both trade and paper, photography, logo and movie design. For her first children's book illustration assignment, *The Piney Woods Peddler,* she spent several months in a stone mill in Pennsylvania which provided the backdrop for the book. Nancy Tafuri enjoys drawing ducks, rabbits, mice, and fairies and making children smile. In 1985 she achieved the Caldecott Honor Award for *Have You Seen My Duckling?* which was also an ALA Notable Book.

BOOK TITLE
Have You Seen My Duckling?
AUTHOR
Nancy Tafuri
ILLUSTRATOR
Nancy Tafuri
PUBLISHER
Greenwillow Books
PUBLICATION DATE
1984
ILLUSTRATION MEDIUM
Watercolor inks, pastels

"*M*oving to the country opened up a whole new way of life, the hills, meadows and farms around us were rich with pictures I wanted to put into my books. One of these focuses was our pond—small but charming and tucked into the meadow's edge it was a perfect backdrop for 'The Duckling'—and when spring brought our resident ducks the story grew right along with our resident family. Have You Seen My Duckling? was my first full-color book without a black line overlay and a thrill to work on from start to finish."

BOOK TITLE
Four Brave Sailors
AUTHOR
Mirra Ginsburg
ILLUSTRATOR
Nancy Tafuri
PUBLISHER
Greenwillow Books
PUBLICATION DATE
1987
ILLUSTRATION MEDIUM
Watercolor inks

"*My editor, Susan Hirschman, called one day with a manuscript by Mirra Ginsburg,* Four Brave Sailors, *for me to consider. I was too excited to wait till it was maïled, so Susan began to read it through and after this line…*

> their ears
> are small and round,
> their coats
> are soft and gray,
> they signal with their tails
> to me
> as they sail away…

I just knew we would all be sailing together!"

BOOK TITLE
Follow Me!
AUTHOR
Nancy Tafuri
ILLUSTRATOR
Nancy Tafuri

PUBLISHER
Greenwillow Books
PUBLICATION DATE
1990
ILLUSTRATION MEDIUM
Watercolor inks

"*While working on* Follow Me! *I was expecting our daughter, Cristina, to whom the book is dedicated. So, it's a very symbolic book even down to the aspect of the mama seal since that's exactly how I felt at the time. But even now as a mother I realize how poignant the book has become to me. Ever watchful, but not interfering as a young pup explores the world around her, and mama being there when she is needed and knowing just what her pup needs to make her happy again.*"

Julie Vivas

Born in Australia, Julie Vivas studied design and architectural drawing and worked in film animation before becoming an illustrator of children's books. In her illustrations she aims for lightness, clear colors, sharp thin line work and simple shapes. She won the Highly Commended Award from the Children's Book Council for her first book, *The Tram to Bondi,* in 1981. Her next book, *Possum Magic,* won an IBBY Honor Diploma, was named a Highly Commended book and was also named Best Children's Book in the 1984 NSW Premier's Literary awards. *The Nativity,* a book she especially enjoyed illustrating, combines artwork with text from the King James version of the Bible.

BOOK TITLE
Possum Magic
AUTHOR
Mem Fox
ILLUSTRATOR
Julie Vivas
PUBLISHER
Omnibus Books, Australia
Harcourt Brace Jovanovich, USA
PUBLICATION DATE
Australia, 1983; USA, 1990
ILLUSTRATION MEDIUM
Watercolor

"*T*he story revolves around an invisible possum and a quest to find the magic that will make her visible. Rendering an invisible character and working with this broken outline was difficult, especially because the other main character is fully rendered in watercolor. It was also difficult showing expressions of sadness or happiness on their faces and through their body language."

"I wanted each page to be resolved as simply as possible, with clean shapes and a dynamic use of space. I found watercolor the best medium to render the fur of the animals and to keep a lightness in the artwork."

"I hoped to draw the reader into the story by creating empathy with the characters and by creating a line of energy and emotion with shapes, colors, and overall design from page to page."

BOOK TITLE
Nurse Lugton's Curtain
AUTHOR
Virginia Woolf
ILLUSTRATOR
Julie Vivas
PUBLISHER
Harcourt Brace Jovanovich
PUBLICATION DATE
1991
ILLUSTRATION MEDIUM
Watercolor

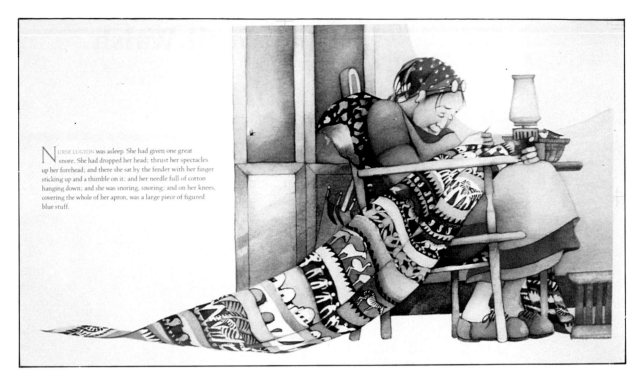

NURSE LUGTON was asleep. She had given one great snore. She had dropped her head; thrust her spectacles up her forehead; and there she sat by the fender with her finger sticking up and a thimble on it; and her needle full of cotton hanging down; and she was snoring, snoring; and on her knees, covering the whole of her apron, was a large piece of figured blue stuff.

"*V*irgina Woolf's text is so descriptive that one feels there is not much need for illustrations, which was a problem in itself. Also problematic was the pattern of the curtain; it felt claustrophobic with the animals trapped in the pattern."

"The transformation of the curtain into landscapes and living animals and people was the most difficult thing to achieve in the book. My aim was to create the illusion that the animals and people were slipping in and out of two worlds."

"I designed the pages so the link was a curving line; the same line structure used in the curtain."

BOOK TITLE
I Went Walking
AUTHOR
Sue Williams
ILLUSTRATOR
Julie Vivas

PUBLISHER
Omnibus Books, Australia
Harcourt Brace Jovanovich, USA
PUBLICATION DATE
Australia, 1989; USA, 1990
ILLUSTRATION MEDIUM
Watercolor

"*T*he main difficulties in this book were the colors, the size differences between the animals and the child, and the procession of animals moving forward and stopping each time a new animal was introduced. This, in particular, posed a problem of arranging the group of animals in the background so the focus was on a half-hidden animal."

"I was aiming to keep up the reader's curiosity, without distracting from the clear, simple text. Design, too, was important; the simpler the text and concept of the book, the tighter the focus is on design."

Richard Jesse Watson

"My formal ar[...]
Maryland Insti[...]
ceived a B.F.A.[...]
1986 Ezra Jack K[...]
Library, Univers[...]
I studied origina[...]
scripts by many[...]
1989 *Mouse Pain*[...]
azine's Reading[...]
chosen as one of[...]
Best Picture Bo[...]

California native Richard Jesse Watson attended Pasadena City College and Art Center College of Design. He became assistant art director for World Vision International and worked as an artist for Hallmark Cards before pursuing a career in freelance children's book illustration. Among his many awards and honors are the Golden Kite Award (1990), Waldenbooks Illustrations Award (1990), Ezra Jack Keats Fellow at the Kerlan Collection of the University of Minnesota, *Parents' Choice* Award for Illustration (1986), Best Book Design from the American Institute of Graphic Arts (1986), and Best Children's Book from the Printing Industries of America.

"*There were a lot of angels that wanted a taste of this cake. I believe in angels and I am sure that they each have unique personalities. So, imperfect as my attempt may have been, I tried to contain at least a feather's glimpse of the heavenly visitors who smelled the young baker's cake all the way from Heaven.*"

BOOK TITLE
The High Rise Glorious Skittle Skat Roarious Sky Pie Angel Food Cake
AUTHOR
Nancy Willard
ILLUSTRATOR
Richard Jesse Watson
PUBLISHER
Harcourt Brace Jovanovich
PUBLICATION DATE
1990
ILLUSTRATION MEDIUM
Egg tempera and neo color pastel

BOOK TITLE
Tom Thumb
AUTHOR
Richard Jesse Watson
ILLUSTRATOR
Richard Jesse Watson
PUBLISHER
Harcourt Brace Jovanovich
PUBLICATION DATE
1989
ILLUSTRATION MEDIUM
Tempera and watercolor

"I love the mystery of small in contrast to big, so this book was a fun adventure. I had a pet mouse in my studio which I used for Tom's trusty steed. I sketched and photographed birds and fish from the Monterey Bay Aquarium. I used neighbors as models, and Merlin I found filling his car at the gas station. Kids always ask me who the giant was. Well, he is a giant, and a friend and a poet named Michael Duffett. Tom was my youngest son, Ben."

David Wiesner

David Wiesner graduated from the Rhode Island School of Design with a B.F.A. in Illustration in 1978. Since that time, he has illustrated over 20 children's books. His paintings have been widely exhibited at galleries and museums, including the Muscarele Museum of Art at the College of William and Mary, the Rhode Island School of Design Museum of Art, the Metropolitan Museum of Art, the Society of Illustrators, and the Brooklyn Public Library. Since 1988, he has been writing as well as illustrating his own books. *Free Fall,* the first book of his own authorship, was awarded a 1989 Caldecott Honor Medal. *The Loathsome Dragon,* which he retold with his wife Kim Kahng, was one of *Redbook* Magazine's Ten Best of 1989. David Wiesner's most recent author/illustrated books are *Hurricane* (1990) and *Tuesday,* winner of the 1992 Caldecott Medal.

BOOK TITLE
Free Fall
AUTHOR
David Wiesner
ILLUSTRATOR
David Wiesner
PUBLISHER
Lothrop, Lee & Shepard
PUBLICATION DATE
1988
ILLUSTRATION MEDIUM
Watercolor

"Free Fall *is a wordless picture book that follows a young boy through the adventures of a night's dream. To evoke the ever-changing nature of a dream, I created a series of metamorphosing landscapes through which the characters walk, float, fly, and ride. Except for the opening and closing images, the pages form one continuous picture. Each reader brings his or her own interpretation to the story."*

BOOK TITLE
Hurricane
AUTHOR
David Wiesner
ILLUSTRATOR
David Wiesner
PUBLISHER
Clarion Books
PUBLICATION DATE
1990
ILLUSTRATION MEDIUM
Watercolor

"Hurricane *is a story that comes from my own childhood. Centering on two brothers, it unfolds in two sections. The first half of the story, which is the dark half, takes place during a severe storm. The scenes are lit by single light sources: a candle, a fireplace, a table lamp. In contrast, the scenes of the second half, which depict the joys of a newly fallen tree, are in bright sunlight. I tried to evoke the warmth and security of the family during the storm, and later, the exuberance of the children at play.*"

BOOK TITLE
Tuesday
AUTHOR
David Wiesner
ILLUSTRATOR
David Wiesner
PUBLISHER
Clarion Books
PUBLICATION DATE
1991
ILLUSTRATION MEDIUM
Watercolor

"Tuesday *continues my exploration of telling stories with pictures. The challenge of the wordless picture book is to effectively utilize every aspect of visual art as a narrative technique. The images are 'read' as carefully as any text.*"

"*I used a varied format for this story. There are pages with multiple small images, full single page pictures, double page spreads, and spreads with panel inserts. I wanted to create a comical mystery, full of slapstick, but with a disquieting mood.*"

Ashley Wolff

BOOK TITLE
A Year of Birds
AUTHOR
Ashley Wolff
ILLUSTRATOR
Ashley Wolff
PUBLISHER
Dodd, Mead & Co.
PUBLICATION DATE
1984
ILLUSTRATION MEDIUM
Linoleum block print and watercolor

"This was my first book and I used the block print technique I developed in art school. This is the lazy printmaker's approach: carve one master block and hand color to avoid the laborious carving of a different block for each color. The story is based on my own childhood and the simplicity of the images helped me put my memories down in a strong, stylized manner."

Photo: Jerry Telfer

Born in Middlebury, Vermont, Ashley Wolff attended Rhode Island School of Design where she majored in illustration and printmaking. She began her career working as an artist for a small newspaper in Marin County, California, and wrote and illustrated her first book, *A Year of Birds,* in 1984 (an ALA Notable Book). *A Year of Beasts* followed in 1988, winning *Parenting* magazine's Reading Magic Award and also being named one of *Redbook's* Ten Best Illustrated Books. Ashley Wolff has illustrated eleven books, four of which she has authored.

BOOK TITLE
Block City
AUTHOR
Robert Louis Stevenson
ILLUSTRATOR
Ashley Wolff

PUBLISHER
Dutton Children's Books
PUBLICATION DATE
1988
ILLUSTRATION MEDIUM
Linoleum block print and watercolor

"I experimented with several other techniques before settling on my established block print style. In the end, that seemed most obvious and appropriate for a story about blocks, where architecture plays such an important part. The contrasts between the 'real' scenes and the 'dream' scenes required using a slightly different palette of watercolors, making the dream scenes warmer, softer and hazier."

BOOK TITLE
Who Is Coming to Our House?
AUTHOR
Joseph Slate
ILLUSTRATOR
Ashley Wolff
PUBLISHER
G.P. Putnam's Sons
PUBLICATION DATE
1988
ILLUSTRATION MEDIUM
**Linoleum block print and
watercolor**

"*I did this book immediately after* Block City *and the two together represent the culmination of my use of this technique to date. I sense a greater reliance on the watercolor and a loosening of the hold of the block prints' outlines. In my next book, I used watercolor exclusively, letting the black line go completely. The block print was effective in presenting the individual animals in a stage-like setting in keeping with the dramatic nature of this story.*"

Don Wood

"The Napping House story is essentially static and repetitive. Very little changes from page to page. The challenge was to transform these qualities, usually considered disadvantages for illustration, into assets."

"I chose to emphasize the repetitive and static nature of the story, rather than trying to liven it up. My vision was that each spread was like a cell in an animated film, therefore the point-of-view changed very slowly as it rose and fell, always maintaining the same comfortable distance from the pile of sleepers."

"The lack of big surprises on each page causes the reader to pay close attention to the subtle changes that do occur, such as a small character making its way onto the scene, or a subtle change of light."

"I had experimented with elaborate cartoons rendered in oils before, but originally thought that The Napping House should have very simple illustrations. Much of the credit for the look of the final art must go to Harcourt Brace Jovanovich's outstanding art director at that time, Rubin Pfeffer, who kept saying 'no, no,' and 'more, more.'"

Illustrator Don Wood earned a B.A. from the University of California, Santa Barbara, in 1967 and an M.F.A. from the California College of Arts and Crafts in 1969. He has worked as a logger, sailmaker and substitute art teacher, and has also owned a book and import shop. He has been an editorial illustrator and graphic designer, as well as an illustrator of children's books. For *The Napping House* he received the Golden Kite Award, the Certificate of Merit from the Society of Illustrators, and the Southern California Council on Literature for Children and Young People Award for significant contribution in illustration. *The Napping House* was also named a *New York Times* Best Illustrated Book of the Year and was a *Booklist* Best of the '80s selection. Another award-winning work, *King Bidgood's in the Bathtub,* garnered a *Parents' Choice* Award, a Certificate of Merit from the Society of Illustrators and a Caldecott Honor Award, among many others. Exhibitions of Don Wood's work include "The Artist as Illustrator," Metropolitan Museum of Art, New York, and the Annual Exhibition of the Society of Illustrators.

BOOK TITLE
The Napping House
AUTHOR
Audrey Wood
ILLUSTRATOR
Don Wood
PUBLISHER
Harcourt Brace Jovanovich
PUBLICATION DATE
1984
ILLUSTRATION MEDIUM
Oils on pressed wood

BOOK TITLE
Heckedy Peg
AUTHOR
Audrey Wood
ILLUSTRATOR
Don Wood
PUBLISHER
Harcourt Brace Jovanovich
PUBLICATION DATE
1987
ILLUSTRATION MEDIUM
Oils on paper

"*I stretched more for* Heckedy Peg *than for any other book I've illustrated. I thought that* Heckedy Peg *was the best story Audrey had written to date, so I was strongly motivated to produce illustrations worthy of it.*"

"Heckedy Peg *reads like an old fairy tale. To emphasize its classic nature, I studied the early seventeenth-century Dutch and Flemish genre painters, especially their use of light. Happily, this was also the correct time frame in which to set the story, so I simultaneously researched the cottages, household effects, and costuming I would need.*"

"*I used photographs of roughly costumed models to paint the characters because the realistic approach I had chosen required so much information. It is, of course, the incredible amount of information that a photograph conveys, that makes it such a potent and dangerous source material. Therefore, one of my main concerns throughout the illustration of* Heckedy Peg, *was that I paint 'people' and not 'photos'.*"

BOOK TITLE
King Bidgood's in the Bathtub
AUTHOR
Audrey Wood
ILLUSTRATOR
Don Wood
PUBLISHER
Harcourt Brace Jovanovich
PUBLICATION DATE
1983
ILLUSTRATION MEDIUM
Oils on pressed wood

"*The premise of* King Bidgood's in the Bathtub *is fantastic. After much soul-searching and experimentation with a broad cartoon style, I finally settled on a much more realistic treatment. I decided that the use of realistic characters, settings and light would contrast excitingly with the fantasy of the story.*"

"*Audrey's manuscript allowed me the pleasure of painting my way through the various times of the day, from dawn to the rising of the full moon. To emphasize the changing light I rendered each illustration first as a monochrome, using a color appropriate to the time of day, then glazed them into full color.*"

"King Bidgood's in the Bathtub *felt operatic to me, so I gave the characters broad gestures and expressions and scattered them over the stage-like setting in outrageous costumes. I pushed the theatrical look of the book to the point of using the bath curtain as a proscenium arch in the closing scenes.*"

Ed Young

Born in Tientsin and raised in Shanghai, China, Ed Young came to the U.S. at age 20, studied architecture at the University of Illinois and graduated from the Art Center School in Los Angeles in 1957. A winner of the 1990 Caldecott Medal for *Lon Po Po,* he has illustrated over 40 children's books, four of which he has also written. *Cats Are Cats* was named one of *The New York Times* Best Illustrated Children's Books in 1988, and *The Emperor and the Kite* was named a Caldecott Honor Book. Ed Young has taught at Pratt Institute, Yale University, Naropa Institute and the University of California at Santa Cruz.

BOOK TITLE
The Emperor and the Kite
AUTHOR
Jane Yolen
ILLUSTRATOR
Ed Young
PUBLISHER
Philomel Books
PUBLICATION DATE
1967, new edition 1988
ILLUSTRATION MEDIUM
Paper-cut, ink, dye

BOOK TITLE
Lon Po Po
AUTHOR
Ed Young
ILLUSTRATOR
Ed Young
PUBLISHER
Philomel Books
PUBLICATION DATE
1989
ILLUSTRATION MEDIUM
Pastel, watercolor

Paul O. Zelinsky

Photo: Deborah Hallen

"For Rumpelstiltskin I wanted to evoke the sense of heightened, but also distanced, reality that I feel looking at paintings from the Renaissance in northern Europe. The sensuous presence I was after—from the crinkliness of straw to the warm shine of gold (which demanded the use of oil glazes over an underpainting) serves, I hope, to set the reader more firmly in the emotional world of the story, and to feel with greater intensity the troubles of the poor miller's daughter, and her eventual release."

Born in Evanston, Illinois, Paul Zelinsky majored in art at Yale College, graduating with a B.A. in 1954. He went on to earn an M.F.A. in painting from Tyler School of Art in Rome and Philadelphia and began illustrating in 1972. His first children's book, *Emily Upham's Revenge,* was published in 1978. He has illustrated 18 children's books, four of which he has written or adapted. Among his many awards are the Caldecott Honor for *Rumpelstiltskin,* 1987, and *Hansel and Gretel,* 1985, and *The New York Times* Best Illustrated Children's Books Award for *The Story of Mrs. Lovewright and Purrless Her Cat,* 1985, and *The Maid and the Mouse and the Odd-shaped House.* His work has been exhibited at the Bratislava Biennale and the Frankfurt Book Fair, as well as at various shows sponsored by the American Institute of Graphic Artists, and the Society of Illustrators.

BOOK TITLE
Rumpelstiltskin
AUTHOR
Adapted from the Brothers Grimm, retold by Paul O. Zelinsky
ILLUSTRATOR
Paul O. Zelinsky
PUBLISHER
Dutton Children's Books
PUBLICATION DATE
1984
ILLUSTRATION MEDIUM
Oil on paper

BOOK TITLE
The Wheels on the Bus
AUTHOR
Adapted by Paul O. Zelinsky
ILLUSTRATOR
Paul O. Zelinsky
PUBLISHER
Dutton Children's Books
PUBLICATION DATE
1990
ILLUSTRATION MEDIUM
**Oil on paper, with some colored
pencil**

"Anyone who knows the song will understand why The Wheels on the Bus *demanded to be illustrated with gusto. Maybe the sound of 'gusto' made me imagine the pictures painted impasto—at any rate, I imagined some kind of pictures you would want to sink your teeth into. It was after much experimentation that I came to the style and technique that seemed right. The paint was not as thick as impasto but it was wet, and scraped into and added onto with colored pencils that would partially melt from the turpentine. The greatest challenge came from the fact that since this was a mechanical book many parts had to be painted separately and apart from their final position, so the organization and balance of the finished book was very iffy and hard to foresee from the original art."*

BOOK TITLE
The Maid and the Mouse and the Odd-shaped House
AUTHOR
Adapted by Paul O. Zelinsky
ILLUSTRATOR
Paul O. Zelinsky

PUBLISHER
Dodd, Mead & Co.
PUBLICATION DATE
1981
ILLUSTRATION MEDIUM
Four-color pre-separated art in gray gouache on acetate; line portion is pen and ink on paper

"*The story in rhyme that was* The Maid and the Mouse *could best be described as wry. The pictures had to evoke the humor in the plight of this pair, whose home remodeling serves to turn their house into a dangerous cat. I made these line drawings filled in with mostly flat but occasionally highly modelled colors to achieve that sense of elegant dignity composed of silly nonsense. The background colors of the pages change in a regular order that also has something to do with the foreground action, evoking, for me, the kind of board game where you move from one colored square to another. I think of this book as a game to be played.*"

BOOK TITLE
A Penny a Look
AUTHOR
Harve Zemach
ILLUSTRATOR
Margot Zemach
PUBLISHER
Farrar, Straus & Giroux
PUBLICATION DATE
1971
ILLUSTRATION MEDIUM
Watercolor ink

BOOK TITLE
It Could Always Be Worse
AUTHOR
Margot Zemach
ILLUSTRATOR
Margot Zemach
PUBLISHER
Farrar, Straus & Giroux
PUBLICATION DATE
1976
ILLUSTRATION MEDIUM
Watercolor ink

Credits

Special appreciation for their invaluable help is extended to the permissions departments of all of the publishers represented in the credits listed below.

10-11 From *In Coal Country* by Judith Hendershot, illustrated by Thomas B. Allen. Illustrations copyright © 1987 by Thomas B. Allen. Reprinted by permission of Alfred A. Knopf, Inc. **12** From *On Granddaddy's Farm* by Thomas B. Allen. Copyright © 1989 by Thomas B. Allen. Reprinted by permission of Alfred A. Knopf, Inc. **13** Illustrations by Mitsumasa Anno reprinted by permission of Philomel Books from *Anno's Medieval World* by Mitsumasa Anno, copyright © 1979 by Kuso-Kobo. **14** Illustrations by Mitsumasa Anno reprinted by permission of Philomel Books from *Topsy-Turvies* by Mitsumasa Anno, copyright © 1968 by Kuso-Kobo. Originally published in Japan by Fukuinkan Shoten, Tokyo in 1968. All rights reserved. **15** Reprinted with permission of Four Winds Press, an imprint of Macmillan Publishing Co. from *Freshwater Fish & Fishing* by Jim Arnosky. Copyright © 1982 by Jim Arnosky. **16** *top* From *Come Out Muskrats* by Jim Arnosky. Copyright © 1989 by Jim Arnosky. Reprinted by permission of Lothrop, Lee & Shepard Books, a division of William Morrow & Company, Inc./Publishers, New York. *bottom* From *Deer at the Brook* by Jim Arnosky. Copyright © 1986 by Jim Arnosky. Reprinted by permission of Lothrop, Lee & Shepard Books, a division of William Morrow & Company, Inc./Publishers, New York. **17** From *The Eleventh Hour* by Graeme Base. Copyright © 1988 by Graeme Base. Used by permission of Penguin Books Australia Ltd. **18-19** From *Animalia* by Graeme Base. Copyright © 1986 by Graeme Base. Used by permission of Penguin Books Australia Ltd. **20** From *The Mousehole Cat*. Text © 1990 Antonia Barber. Illustrations © 1990 Nicola Bayley. Published in the UK by Walker Books Ltd. Reprinted by permission of Walker Books Ltd. Reprinted with permission of Macmillan Publishing Co. from *The Mousehole Cat* by Nicola Bayley. Copyright © 1990 by Nicola Bayley. **21** From *Quentin Blake's ABC* by Quentin Blake. Copyright © 1989 by Quentin Blake. Reprinted by permission of Alfred A. Knopf, Inc., New York, and Jonathan Cape, London. **22** *top* From *Mrs. Armitage on Wheels* by Quentin Blake. Copyright © 1987 by Quentin Blake. Reprinted by permission of Alfred A. Knopf, Inc., New York and Jonathan Cape, London. *bottom* From *Mister Magnolia* by Quentin Blake. Copyright © 1980 by Quentin Blake. Reprinted by permission of Jonathan Cape, London. **23** Illustrations by Jan Brett reprinted by permission of G.P. Putnam's Sons from *The Owl and the Pussycat* by Edward Lear, illustrations copyright © 1991 by Jan Brett. **24** Illustrations by Jan Brett reprinted by permission of G.P. Putnam's Sons from *The Mitten*, copyright © 1989 by Jan Brett. **25** Illustrations by Jan Brett reprinted by permission of G.P. Putnam's Sons from *The Wild Christmas Reindeer*, copyright © 1990 by Jan Brett. **26** From *Rabbit Inn* by Patience Brewster. Copyright © 1991 by Patience Brewster. Reprinted with permission of Little, Brown and Company. **27** *top* From *Bear and Mrs. Duck* by Elizabeth Winthrop. Text copyright © 1988 by Elizabeth Winthrop. Illustrations copyright © 1988 by Patience Brewster. Reprinted by permission of Holiday House. *bottom* From *Princess Abigail & The Wonderful Hat* by Steven Kroll. Text copyright © 1991 by Steven Kroll. Illustrations copyright © 1991 by Patience Brewster. Reprinted by permission of Holiday House. **28** Illustrations by Eric Carle reprinted by permission of Philomel Books from *The Very Hungry Caterpillar*, copyright © 1969 by Eric Carle. **29** *top* Illustrations by Eric Carle reprinted by permission of Philomel Books from *Eric Carle's Animals, Animals*, copyright © 1989 by Eric Carle. *bottom* Illustrations by Eric Carle reprinted by permission of Philomel Books from *The Very Quiet Cricket*, copyright © 1990 Eric Carle. **30** From *Dylan's Day Out* by Peter Catalanotto. Copyright © 1989 by Peter Catalanotto for illustrations. Used by permission of Orchard Books, New York. **31** From *Mr. Mumble* by Peter Catalanotto. Copyright © 1990 by Peter Catalanotto for illustrations. Used by permission of Orchard Books, New York. **32** From *Cecil's Story* by George Ella Lyon, illustrations by Peter Catalanotto. Copyright © 1991 by Peter Catalanotto for illustrations. Used by permission of Orchard Books, New York. **33** Illustrations from *Froggie Went A-Courting* retold with pictures by Chris Conover. Copyright © 1986 by Chris Conover. Reproduced by permission of Farrar, Straus & Giroux, Inc. **34** *top* Illustrations from *Mother Goose and the Sly Fox* retold with pictures by Chris Conover. Copyright © 1989 Chris Conover. Reproduced by permission of Farrar, Straus & Giroux, Inc. *bottom* Illustrations from *Six Little Ducks*, copyright © 1976 by Chris Conover. Reprinted by permission of Chris Conover. **35** From *Ox-Cart Man* by Donald Hall, illustrated by Barbara Cooney. Copyright © 1979 by Barbara Cooney Porter for illustrations. Used by permission of Viking Penguin, a division of Penguin Books USA, Inc. **36** From *Roxaboxen* by Alice McLerran. Text copyright © 1991 by Alice McLerran. Illustrations copyright © 1991 by Barbara Cooney. Reprinted by permission of Lothrop, Lee & Shepard, a division of William Morrow & Co. Inc./Publishers, New York. **37** From *Miss Rumphius* by Barbara Cooney. Copyright © 1982 by Barbara Cooney Porter. Used by permission of Viking Penguin, a division of Penguin Books USA, Inc. **38** From *Carousel* by Donald Crews. Copyright © 1982 by Donald Crews. Reprinted by permission of Greenwillow Books, a division of William Morrow & Co., Inc./Publishers, New York. **39** From *Truck* by Donald Crews. Copyright © 1980 by Donald Crews. Reprinted by permission of Greenwillow Books, a division of William Morrow & Co., Inc./Publishers, New York. **40** *top* From *Flying* by Donald Crews. Copyright © 1986 by Donald Crews. Reprinted by permission of Greenwillow Books, a division of William Morrow & Co., Inc./Publishers, New York. *bottom* From *Freight Train* by Donald Crews. Copyright © 1978 by Donald Crews. Reprinted by permission of Greenwillow Books, a division of William Morrow & Co., Inc./Publishers, New York. **41** Illustrations from *Storm in the Night*. Written by Mary Stolz, illustrated by Pat Cummings. Copyright © 1988 by Pat Cummings. Reprinted by permission of HarperCollins Publishers. **42** *top* From *C.L.O.U.D.S.* by Pat Cummings. Copyright © 1986 by Pat Cummings. Reprinted by permission of Lothrop, Lee & Shepard Books, a division of William Morrow & Co., Inc./Publishers, New York. *bottom* Illustrations from *I Need A Lunch Box*. Written by Jeanette Caines, illustrated by Pat Cummings. Copyright © 1988 by Pat Cummings. Reprinted by permission of HarperCollins Publishers. **43** Illustrations by Tomie dePaola reprinted by permission of G.P. Putnam's Sons from *Tomie dePaola's Mother Goose*, copyright © 1985 by Tomie dePaola. **44-45** Illustrations by Tomie dePaola reprinted by permission of G.P. Putnam's Sons from *Tony's Bread*, copyright © 1989 by Tomie dePaola. *bottom* Illustrations by Tomie dePaola reprinted by permission of G.P. Putnam's Sons from *The Legend of the Bluebonnet*, copyright © 1983 by Tomie dePaola. **46** From *Simon's Book* by Henrik Drescher. Copyright © 1983 by Henrik Drescher. Reprinted by permission of Lothrop, Lee & Shepard Books, a division of William Morrow & Company, Inc./Publishers, New York. **47** *top* *Looking for Santa Claus* by Henrik Drescher. Copyright © 1984 by Henrik Drescher. Published by Lothrop, Lee & Shepard, a division of William Morrow & Company, Inc./Publishers, New York. Reprinted by permission from Henrik Drescher. *bottom* *The Strange Appearance of Howard Cranebill, Jr.* by Henrik Drescher. Copyright © 1982 by Henrik Drescher. Published by Lothrop, Lee & Shepard, a division of William Morrow & Company, Inc./Publishers, New York. Reprinted by permission from Henrik Drescher. **48** Illustrations from *The Tub People*. Written by Pam Conrad and illustrated by Richard Egielski. Copyright © 1989 by Richard Egielski. Reprinted by permission of HarperCollins Publishers. **49** *top* Illustrations from *Hey, Al* by Arthur Yorinks with pictures by Richard Egielski. Pictures copyright © 1986 by Richard Egielski. Reproduced by permission of Farrar, Straus, and Giroux Inc. *bottom* Illustrations from *Oh, Brother* by Arthur Yorinks with pictures by Richard Egielski. Pictures copyright © 1986 by Richard Egielski. Reproduced by permission of Farrar, Straus, and Giroux Inc. **50** Illustrations from *Color Zoo*, copyright © 1989 by Lois Ehlert. Reprinted by permission of HarperCollins Publishers. **51** *top* Illustrations from *Eating the Alphabet: Fruits and Vegetables from A to Z*, copyright © 1989 by Lois Ehlert, reprinted by permission of Harcourt Brace Jovanovich, Inc. *bottom* Illustrations from *Feathers for Lunch*, copyright © 1990 by Lois Ehlert, reprinted by permission of Harcourt Brace Jovanovich, Inc. **52** *top* *Chicka Chicka Boom Boom* by Bill Martin, Jr. and John Archambault—illustrated by Lois Ehlert copyright © 1989. Reprinted by permission of the publisher, Simon & Schuster Books for Young Readers, New York, NY. *bottom* Illustrations from *Fish Eyes*, copyright © 1990 by Lois Ehlert, reprinted by permission of Harcourt Brace Jovanovich, Inc. **53** Reprinted with permission of Macmillan Publishing Company from *The ABC Exhibit* by Leonard Everett Fisher. Copyright © 1991 by Leonard Everett Fisher. **54** From *Space Songs* by Myra Cohn Livingston. Text copyright © 1988 by Myra Cohn Livingston. Illustrations copyright © 1988 by Leonard Everett Fisher. Reprinted with permission of Holiday House. **55** *top* Reprinted with permission of Macmillan Publishing Company from *Prince Henry the Navigator* by Leonard Everett Fisher. Copyright © 1990 by Leonard Everett Fisher. *bottom* Reprinted with permission of Macmillan Publishing Company from *Pyramid of the Sun, Pyramid of the Moon* by Leonard Everett Fisher. Copyright © 1988 by Leonard Everett Fisher. **56** *top* From *What's In Fox's Sack?* retold by Paul Galdone. Copyright © 1982 by Paul Galdone. Reprinted by permission of Clarion Books, a Houghton Mifflin Company imprint. All rights reserved. *bottom* From *Rumpelstiltskin* retold by Paul Galdone. Copyright © 1985 by Paul Galdone. Reprinted by permission of Clarion Books, a Houghton Mifflin Company imprint. All rights reserved. **57** From *Oink* by Arthur Geisert, copyright © 1991 by Arthur Geisert. Reprinted by permission of Houghton Mifflin Company. All rights reserved. **58** From *Pigs A to Z* by Arthur Geisert, copyright © 1986 by Arthur Geisert. Reprinted by permission of Houghton Mifflin Company. All rights reserved. **59** Illustrations from *Rosie and the Rustlers* by Roy Gerrard, copyright © 1988 by Roy Gerrard. Reprinted by permission of Victor Gollancz Ltd., London, and Farrar Straus & Giroux, New York. **60** *top* Illustrations from *Sir Cedric* by Roy Gerrard, copyright © 1984 by Roy Gerrard. Reprinted by permission of Victor Gollancz Ltd., London, and Farrar Straus & Giroux, New York. *bottom* Illustrations from *Sir Francis Drake* by Roy Gerrard, copyright © 1988 by Roy Gerrard. Reprinted by permission of Victor Gollancz Ltd., London, and Farrar Straus & Giroux, New York. **61** From *When I Was Young in the Mountains* by Cynthia Rylant, illustrated by Diane Goode. Copyright © 1982 by Diane Goode for illustrations. Used by permission of Dutton Children's Books, a division of Penguin Books USA, Inc. **62** From *Watch the Stars Come Out* by Riki Levinson, illustrated by Diane Goode. Copyright © 1985 by Diane Goode for illustrations. Used by permission of Dutton Children's Books, a division of Penguin Books USA, Inc. **63** *top* From *Where's Our Mama?* by Diane Goode. Copyright © 1991 by Diane Goode. Used by permission of Dutton Children's Books, a division of Penguin Books, USA. *bottom* From *I Go With My Family To Grandma's* by Riki Levinson, illustrated by Diane Goode. Copyright © 1986 by Diane Goode for illustrations. Used by permission of Dutton Children's Books, a division of Penguin Books USA, Inc. **64-65** From *The Village of Round and Square Houses* by Ann Grifalconi. Copyright © 1986 by Ann Grifalconi. Reprinted with permission of Little, Brown and Company. **66** Reprinted with permission of Margaret K. McElderry Books, an imprint of Macmillan Publishing Co. from *The Most Wonderful Egg in the World* written and illustrated by Helme Heine. Copyright © 1983 Gertraud Middelhauve Verlag, Koln. **67** Reprinted with permission of Margaret K. McElderry Books, an imprint of Macmillan Publishing Co. from *Friends* written and illustrated by Helme Heine. Copyright © 1982 Gertraud Middelhauve Verlag, Koln. **68** From *Julius, The Baby of the World* by Kevin Henkes. Copyright © 1990 by Kevin Henkes. Reprinted by permission of Greenwillow Books, a division of William Morrow & Company, Inc./Publishers, New York. **69** *top* From *Chester's Way* by Kevin Henkes. Copyright © 1988 by Kevin Henkes. Reprinted by permission of Greenwillow Books, a division of William Morrow & Company, Inc./Publishers, New York. *bottom* From *Jessica* by Kevin Henkes. Copyright © 1989 by Kevin Henkes. Reprinted by permission of Greenwillow Books, a division of William Morrow & Company, Inc./Publishers, New York. **70** Reprinted with permission of Macmillan Publishing Co. From *The Dakota Dugout* by Ann Turner. Illustrated by Ronald Himler. Illustrations copyright © 1985 by Ronald Himler. **71** From *The Wall* by Eve Bunting, illustrated by Ronald Himler. Illustrations copyright © 1991 by Ronald Himler. Reprinted by permission of Clarion Books, a Houghton Mifflin Company imprint. **72** From *Fly Away Home* by Eve Bunting, illustrated by Ronald Himler. Illustrations copyright © 1990 by Ronald Himler. Reprinted by permission of Clarion Books, a Houghton Mifflin Company imprint. **73** Reprinted with permission of Macmillan Publishing Co. from *Rosie's Walk* by Pat Hutchins.

234

Author/Illustrator Index

Title Index